Designs For Cottage And Villa Architecture...

Samuel H Brooks

DESIGNS

FOR

COTTAGE AND VILLA ARCHITECTURE;

CONTAINING

PLANS, ELEVATIONS, SECTIONS,

PERSPECTIVE VIEWS, AND DETAILS,

FOR THE

ERECTION OF COTTAGES AND VILLAS.

By S. H. BROOKS, Esq.,

ARCHITECT.

LONDON:

THOMAS KELLY, PATERNOSTER ROW,

AND SOLD BY ALL BOOKSELLERS.

INTRODUCTION.

ENGLAND has been justly designated a cultivated garden; and, perhaps, in no particular does she possess a greater pre-eminence over the other European nations than in the beauty and neatness of her rural edifices, whether they be considered as specimens of architectural skill, as objects of ornament, or as dwellings adapted for the general purposes of life, on the best and most acknowledged principles of utility, comfort, and economy. An Englishman, when he first travels on the Continent, with every disposition to discover and confirm the superiority of his own country, particularly remarks, as one of the causes of that superiority, the comparatively small number of suburban villas which are to be seen in the vicinity of even the largest towns, and which form such a delightful feature in the landscape scenery of England. On minute inquiry, he finds that this difference arises from the peculiar habits and character of the people; and that a German, who has realized an independence by trade, or any other pursuit, instead of retiring into the country to enjoy it, removes from a small town or village, in which the fortune was made, to a larger one; whereas, it is the exact reverse with an Englishman, in whose mind the idea of retirement from business and a country life are inseparably united: and thus, *par eminence*, England becomes the country of suburban villas.

The architectural style of the dwellings of the different classes of society is certainly an object of great importance, and every attempt towards the improvement of it is worthy of serious consideration. The efforts of architects in all ages have hitherto been generally directed to public buildings, and to the mansions of noblemen; and those who may be considered as composing the middling orders of society have been for the most part left to become their own architects. Hence the tardiness with which the improvements made in the accommodation, arrangement, and exterior beauty of the mansions of the wealthy have found their way to the dwellings of the middling classes. It is therefore one of the chief objects of the present work, to point out by appropriate designs, how the residence of the man of wealth, and the dwellings of a more humble grade, may in a degree, be equalized as far as regards essential comfort, convenience, and beauty.

A series of published designs cannot but prove of great benefit, not only to the experienced, but also to the amateur architect; for the first step towards the introduction of improvement in the practice of any art, is to familiarize the minds of the practitioners with the deviations from usual practice, which may be considered as the foundation of those improvements. In rural architecture, particularly, the only means of accomplishing that end, is the study of published designs, for no local builder can be supposed to have had either leisure or opportunity to inspect the different improvements which have gradually or immediately taken place in his own country, or which may be the result of foreign talent. Without recourse to a book of designs, the builder must in his own plans be necessarily tame and uniform, his edifices will be but a copy of each other, and that which he intended for an improvement, may, in reality, be a deformity.

A most important advantage may be derived from the details of construction which accompany the designs; and the practical utility of this department of the work must necessarily carry with it its own recommendation, inasmuch as it is not only the best adapted for initiating the young architect in the principles of architectural taste, but it also furnishes him with the means of making use of the specified improvements which it is one of the objects of the present work to introduce.

It is an acknowledged fact, that many persons are deterred from entering upon the erection of a villa or other buildings from a want of knowledge of the expense to be incurred. Each design, therefore, will be accompanied by an estimate of the gross expense for which the building may be erected. It must also be considered as a valuable feature of this work, that every builder, when he has had laid before him one of these designs, with the specification of the details of construction, will always be able to form an estimate suitable for contract or actual execution.

In regard to the different styles of architecture which are displayed in the designs of the present work, much must be necessarily left to the taste of the projector, as one may prefer a mixed style of architecture, while another gives the preference to the pure Grecian, Italian, Tudor, or Elizabethan, and in this respect the fashion of the day possesses no little influence.

By a practical application of the principles contained in the following pages, and a strict attention to the details and other minutiæ, which are designedly given for the uninitiated in the science of architecture or the art of building, many of the obstacles will be removed which at present stand in the way of the erection of our suburban villas, whilst at the same time, the exterior beauty of the edifice will be improved, with a corresponding increase of interior comfort, convenience, and utility.

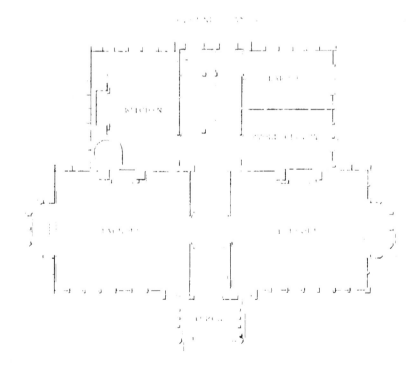

SPECIFICATION AND DETAILS

OF

DESIGNS FOR

COTTAGES AND VILLAS.

———•———

COMMENCING with the more simple style of architecture, *Plate* I. consists of a perspective view, and the ground plan for a cottage, constructed in the old English style of domestic architecture, consisting of two parlours, kitchen, larder, store-room, and water-closet, on the ground-floor, and three bed-rooms on the chamber-floor: this method of erection, combined with the present improved and scientific state of building, may be very properly and economically introduced in any isolated situation where picturesque outline may be a desideratum. The building is constructed with framed quarterings, properly and securely fixed upon a stone or brick plinth, and brick nogging to be introduced between the said quarterings, the inside to be properly plastered, and the outside between the quarterings also plastered and rough cast; or, a more lasting and substantial method would be, to *render the outside* with cement, and paint it; the whole of the timbers to be coloured, in imitation of oak, with a composition of coal tar and Roman ochre. The terrace is a matter of secondary consideration, and must entirely depend upon the locality of the situation; the building being complete without it. It is purposed to pave the porch, passages, and water-closet, with York paving; and the kitchen, larder, and store-room, with red paving-tiles; the floor-joist of the parlours to be $4\frac{1}{2}$ inches × 2 inches, properly notched on, and nailed to oak sleepers, bedded on brickwork at proper distances; the floors to be of $1\frac{1}{4}$ inch yellow deal; the architraves to doors, &c., will be merely champhered on each edge, to correspond with the skirting and panelling

C

of room, for which, see the sheet of detail. The joist for chamber-floor to be 9 inches × 2½ inches, sound boarded and pugged between, well notched and securely nailed to the wall-plates; the floor to be laid with one-inch yellow deal; the doors for this floor, with the architraves, &c., will finish similar to those below. The frame of the roof being small will not require principals, but couples and collar pieces at proper distances; purloins, 5 inches × 4 inches; couples, 5 inches × 3 inches; common rafters, 3½ inches × 2 inches; hips and valleys, 6 inches × 2 inches, the whole properly and well secured to the wall-plate, &c. This cottage, according to the accompanying drawings, when completely finished, with every requisite, may be erected for the sum of £350.

Plate II.—Shows a longitudinal section and chamber plan.

Plate III.—Elucidates the various details applicable to the following figures:

Figure 1.—Shows the method of framing and securing the angular posts into the principal wall-plates of the building.

A A. Principal wall-plates.

B B. Angular posts.

D D. Iron straps, which should be ½ inch by 2½, and properly potted and screwed as is shown in the sketch.

Figure 2.—Indicates the manner of fixing the angular posts into the stone.

C C. Stone.

B B. Angular post.

Figure 3.—Explains the method of bedding the wood sill upon the stone plinth, and attaching it, by means of a tenon, to the angular posts, which are to be secured by an iron bolt let through the angular parts into the sills; the other portion shows the manner of stubbing the smaller quarterings into the sill.

It is requisite that a sheet of lead rather larger than the size of the plinth should be placed upon the stone, so that any vacuum that may arise from

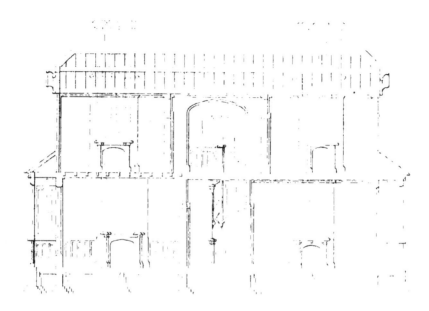

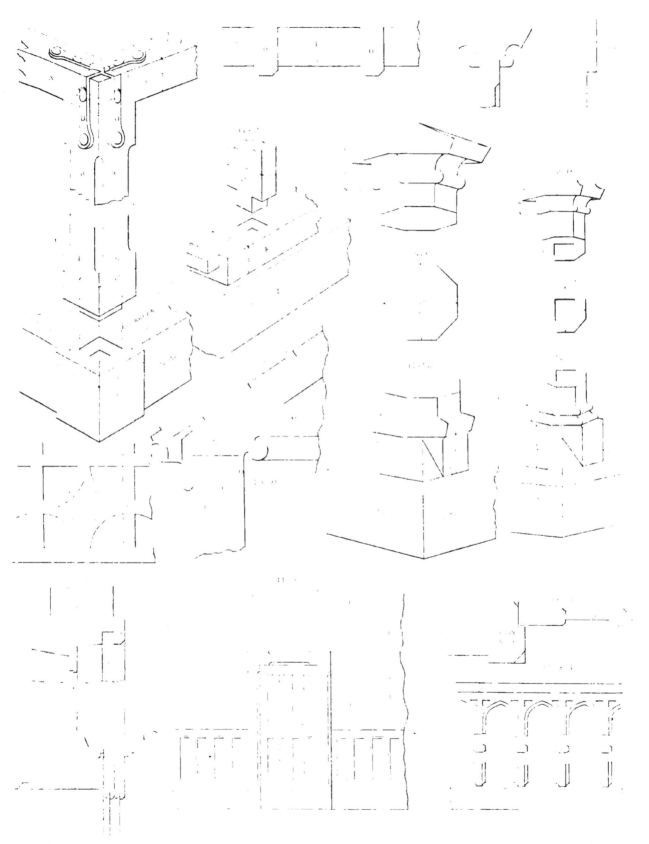

the inaccuracy of the workman may become air-tight, and prevent the water lodging in the cavity.

E. Stone plinth.

F. Wood sill.

G. Strutt or quartering.

Figure 4.—Is a plan of the construction of the quarterings, brick nogging, plastering, rough casting, &c.

H H. Upright quarterings.

I. Brick nogging.

J. Plastering.

K. Plastering and rough casting.

Figure 5.—Is a plan of the angular posts of entrance porch.

Figure 6.—Shows a sketch of the mouldings of top of the same.

Figure 7.—Indicates the base, and the method of fixing it in the stone plinth.

Figure 8.—A plan of one of the chimney-pots.

Figure 9.—Elevation of top of the same.

Figure 10.—Elevation of base of ditto.

Figure 11.—A section of a portion of the roof, showing the form of zinc gutter, &c.

L. Rafter.

M. Ceiling joists.

N. Wall-plate.

O. Brick nogging.

P. Gutter.

Q. Plastering.

R. Plaster and rough casting, or cement outside.

S. Slates.

Figure 12 shows the method of applying the segmentical pieces, which are merely pieces an inch thick nailed to the horizontal and vertical quarterings.

T. Sill.

U. Horizontal quartering.

V. Vertical quartering.

W. Segmentical pieces.

Figure 13.—Head of the bay window.

X. Brick nogging.

Y. Plastering.

Z. Head.

* Iron casement. A new method of fixing and applying the metal casement has been introduced, those in general use not being air or water tight.

III. Architrave.

IIII. Space for shutters.

Figure 14.—Sill of bay window.

Figure 15.—Door and frame, with panelling, skirting, &c., for principal room.

Figure 16.—Plan of ditto, showing the method of applying the fillets to form small panels.

Figure 17.—Plan and elevation of head and sill of entrance porch.

Figure 18.—Hand rail, and banister of stairs.

Figure 19.—Skirting of principal room.

PRELIMINARY REMARKS,

AS TO SITUATION, &c.

———◆———

PREVIOUSLY to entering upon a specification of the details of the designs contained in this work, it will not be considered either uninteresting or unprofitable to enter upon an exposition of those preliminary and very important points which ought to be taken into mature consideration before the resolution be finally adopted to erect a dwelling on any given site.

In the erection of every dwelling, destined as a human habitation, the selection of a wholesome and suitable situation is of primary importance; and it is the culpable inattention to this prudential rule which is the cause of so much subsequent disappointment, and ultimately disheartening the proprietor from prosecuting those improvements which may have subsequently been found necessary to establish or increase the comfort and convenience of the newly erected residence. An extensive prospect is certainly a very great desideratum in the choice of a situation, but the most delightful views will not compensate for the absence of several other essential advantages and indispensable comforts, without which no dwelling can be said to be complete, nor, in some degree, even habitable. A damp situation is, of all others, to be avoided; for no beauty of style, nor taste in the ornamental departments, nor judgment in the construction of the requisite conveniences, can, in any degree, compensate for those evils which are the invariable results of a low and damp situation. Health, which is one of the primary objects to be maintained, and perhaps obtained by the erection of a country residence, becomes daily and hourly sacrificed, independently of the injury which is imperceptibly committed on the interior decorations, the furniture, and wearing apparel. A continual system

B

of repair is required, and one injury or dilapidation has been no sooner remedied, than another presents itself, which has been insidiously creeping upon the premises, on account of the dampness of the situation. The nature of the soil, the sub-soil, and the character of the surface, should, therefore, be the first objects of examination in the selection of an appropriate site for a dwelling; a light gravelly soil, on account of its porosity, is to be preferred to one of a thick, tenacious clay, which, on account of its strong adhesive power, prevents the filtration of the water, and thereby imparts a continual dampness to a dwelling, which renders it both offensive and unwholesome. The vicinity of marshy and stagnant waters is a very injudicious site for a dwelling; for, independently of the malaria which issue from those waters, especially in summer, they create an atmospheric dampness, which communicates itself to the surrounding dwellings, and is the great cause of epidemical diseases.

The partial or general degree of exposure of the building is another material point to be taken into consideration. A house that is wholly unsheltered, particularly from the north and the east, can never be suitable for the habitation of a family, especially if composed of children. Art may indeed accomplish much in the removal of the defects of a too open exposure; but, as trees are the best and most ornamental shelter, it must be taken into consideration, that the remedy is of a very slow and dilatory nature, and, consequently, that all the evil may be committed before the remedy can be brought into actual operation. It becomes, therefore, an art of no minor importance, to consider well the greater or less exposure of the situation, before it be finally determined upon as the site of a country residence.

The aspect of a house is in a great degree connected with the exposure; for it not unfrequently happens, that in order to obtain the one the other becomes necessarily sacrificed; for, to ensure the requisite shelter, the aspect of a house is made a subordinate consideration; and thus, that which is one of the greatest recommendations of a dwelling is treated as of minor importance, or wholly neglected, with the view of obtaining a merely secondary advantage. Climate has, certainly, a considerable influence on the choice of the aspect of a dwelling; for that which would be advisable in England, would be deemed an injudicious choice in the more southern countries of Europe. The south, or the south-east, is the most proper aspect for an English dwelling, and which, amongst others, possesses the great advantage of enabling the builder to give a northern aspect to some of the offices, such as the dairy, the pantry, the cellar, &c. The most wholesome aspect for a bed-room is decidedly the south-east; and, to a valetudinarian, the northern is the most injurious. The architectural excellence of a house will, therefore, in a great measure, depend upon the greater or less degree of judgment shown in the choice of the aspect of the habitable rooms; but it is certain that those who have not had much experience in the choice of a house are, generally, more captivated with the appearance of the exterior, than with the existence of those positive advantages, without which no dwelling can be said to be complete, nor to possess the requisite comfort and convenience.

The facility with which water can be obtained, as well as the component character, are no trifling considerations in the selection of a situation. There cannot, perhaps, possibly exist a greater drawback to the value of a house than a supply of bad water, or a scarcity of it when it is good. There are some departments in the domestic arrangements of a family to which rain-water is inapplicable; nor, when applicable, can a regular supply of it be always depended upon. The health of a family is greatly dependent upon the nature of the water which they consume, and, consequently, an inattention to this very important point in the choice of a situation for a residence has proved the after-cause of universal dissatisfaction, if not of the abandonment of the premises altogether.

An English cottage is proverbially characteristic of internal comfort and exterior neatness; it must however be observed, that in the style of architecture adopted by our forefathers in the erection of their country dwellings, a taste for picturesque beauty was very little consulted, and a uniform and monotonous character imparted to them, which appeared rather as blotches than ornaments to our landscape scenery. It ought therefore to be the aim and business of the young architect, not only to inform himself in all that relates to actual fitness in a building, and in whatever contributes to the expression of purpose, but also to those circumstances in style which are calculated to operate on the imagination. With this view, the accompanying designs are intended to exhibit to what extent the improvements in our rural edifices may be applied to even the smallest dwellings, and how, with all or any of those ameliorations, the various degrees of architectural style or beauty may be produced in cottages. It is evident, that to introduce irregularity of form in buildings is an architectural refinement of the present age; and it is not less certain that irregular buildings please the admirers, partly with reference to their picturesque effect, and partly as being characteristic of some particular architectural style, as it is found to exist in ancient buildings. The castellated architecture of the present day is evidently more an imitative style than one of picturesque beauty, and the irregular cottage style depends more on its picturesqueness than on its being an imitation of any thing that has previously existed. It will however be seen, by a strict examination of the designs contained in this work, that in the selection and combination of the different styles, care has been taken to preserve the picturesque character of the edifice, with every requisite attention to comfort, convenience, and economy.

The art of arranging villas in England is far better understood than the construction of cottages; the reason of this is, that the occupants of the latter description of residence have hitherto been deficient in that degree of cultivation which is necessary to the display of what is considered good taste, and have neglected to call in the assistance of the taste of professional men. The occupiers of villas, on the contrary, have not only possessed more cultivation and taste than the others, but, from their wealth, have been able to command the services of all who possessed an ability to render them assistance. Hence it has followed, that the villas of England, though different in some particulars, are yet decidedly superior to those of every other country. It is, however, for the purpose of removing the impediments which exist in the way of obtaining the practical assistance of scientific men, and of obviating the attendant expense, that the present work has been projected. By a simple examination of the designs, details, &c., with a correct estimate of the expense, the individual projecting the erection of a cottage or villa, can render himself at once master of the subject; he can be his own overseer; and, with the practical instructions laid before him, he becomes a judge of the fitness of the execution, and absolves himself from the possibility of imposition.

The next plate, IV. exhibits a design for a double cottage, in the Ionic style of architecture; each dwelling containing a kitchen, back kitchen, larder, and water-closet, on the basement floor; dining-room and drawing-room on the ground floor; and two bed-rooms and a dressing-room on the chamber floor.

The basement story is purposed to be 9 feet high from floor line to ceiling; the kitchen 16 feet by 14 feet; back kitchen or scullery 14 feet by 12 feet 6 inches. A larder under the hall 10 feet by 7 feet 6 inches; and a water-closet 5 feet × 3 feet. The dotted line below the ground on this elevation, shows the depth it is intended to carry the various foundations, which if erected on a damp soil, or a loose earthy stratum, should be filled in with concrete, mixed in the proportion of one-fourth of lime and three-fourths of clean gravel, and thrown into the trenches, while warm. The trench must be excavated to a depth according to the description of soil; for instance, on a clayey soil it would not be necessary to use concrete, but on a loose earth it would be necessary to concrete to the depth of from 12 to 18 or even 24 inches, according to the weight of the building.

Figure 1.—Principal, or entrance elevation.

Figure 2.—Ground plan.

This story is purposed to be 10 feet 6 inches high, and to ascend from the ground line to the floor line 2 feet, which is accomplished by 4 steps of 6 inches rise each, introducing you to a small hall, 13 feet by 8 feet; in immediate communication with which, and facing the entrance, are the stairs, which might, if greater seclusion be the object, be divided from the hall, by means of a slight partition. From the hall, or principal passage, you enter the drawing-room or back parlour communicating with each other by means of suspended folding doors, which, from the method of construction, that will be more fully explained in a future part of this work, will be found to be more desirable than any other plan hitherto introduced to the notice of the public, in consequence of the sound, when it becomes necessary to divide the rooms, being entirely prevented from passing from one room to the other. The dimensions of the drawing-room are 17 ft. by 15 ft.; the parlour 15 ft. by 13 ft. Over this story it will be requisite to sound-board, and pug the floors, which is accomplished at a comparatively small expense, considering the comfort that is derived from it; as nothing can be more annoying than an apartment, with the slightest pretensions to domestic comfort, in which the sound is heard passing over head. The bed-rooms will be nearly of the same dimensions as the rooms below, with a dressing-room over the hall. The rooms in the roof may be appropriated to the use of the servants.

Plate V.

Figure 3.—Is an elevation, answering to the same plan, and in the same style of architecture; but, in design, much plainer, and, consequently, less expensive.

Figure 4.—On the same plate, introduces an elevation in the Tudor or mixed style of old English cottage architecture; being also applicable to the same plan in regard to arrangement.

The selection of either of these designs must entirely depend upon the taste of the parties intending to erect them; and the appearance of the building, when executed, will be considerably improved by the surrounding objects or scenery being in keeping with the style adopted. The Ionic style, which is exhibited in the plates 4 and 5, is, on account of its simplicity, the best adapted for suburban cottages, as in the environs of the metropolis, little of that grandeur or sub-limity of locality can be found, which would sanction the adoption of the Gothic, or the castellated architecture of the present day; in, fact one of the greatest proofs of the skill of the architect, is the adaptation of the style of the erection to the character of the surrounding scenery, thereby avoiding those incongruities and monstrosities which grossly disfigure many of the lately-erected edifices. It is purposed to build the two classical erections (figures 1, 2, and, ground plan, 3) with bricks, and to execute all the embellishments in Roman cement, and stone only where it becomes absolutely requisite; the basement floor to be paved with rough York flags; joists for ground-floor to be 9 inches × 2½ inches; trimmers 9 inches × 3 inches, and covered with 1¼-inch yellow deal floor boards. The chamber-floor to have joists of the same scantling, and boards of a similar description. The roofs to these buildings will require no principal rafters, as the common rafters will fix upon the pole-plate and a ridge-plate that will be bedded upon the division wall; it will, however, be requisite to have a couple of tie-beams to run across, resting upon each external flank wall of the principal building, cogged, and properly secured, and fixed to the wall-plates, which plates

ELEVATION

OPEN

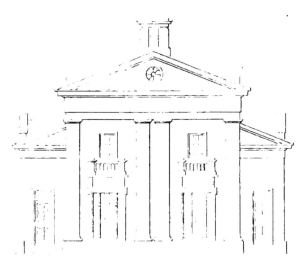

ELEVATION

FIG IV

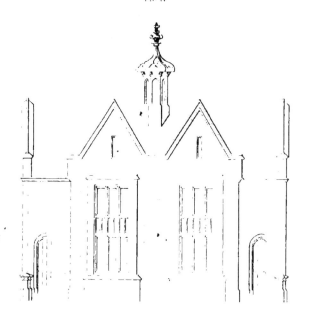

must run all round the building, and be securely scarfed, halved, and dove-tailed at the angles. It is intended for the two small wings to have flats; the principal roof may be covered with slates, and the wings with suitable lead, marine metal, or zinc. The scantling of the timbers for the roofs may be as follows:—wall-plates, 6 inches × 4½ inches; tie-beams, 10 inches × 4 inches; pole-plate, 4 inches × 4 inches; purloins, 5 inches × 4 inches; ridge-piece, 6 inches × 2 inches; common rafters, 3½ inches × 2 inches; ceiling joists, 3 inches × 2 inches; strutts, 3 inches × 2 inches; joists for wings, 5 inches × 2 inches; bond timber, 4½ inches × 3 inches. The chamber plan will be sound-boarded and pugged. The inside finishing of these houses should be kept as nearly consistent with the general costume of the buildings as possible; but, as a great deal depends upon the taste and fancy of the party building, without materially altering the expense, it may be, perhaps, judicious not to enlarge further on the subject. The elevation (figure 4) is intended to be built with bricks or flints, with stone quoins, coping, plinth, jambs and mullions of windows.

The turret, which is a general receiver of smoke from the various flues, and forms a prominent feature in this building, must also be of stone. The method of adapting this for its intended purpose, and which I have executed with great success, is, by conducting the smoke into a small chamber, constructed immediately under the base of the turret, and which acts by means of valves, over which is placed an iron fly, similar to that of a smoke-jack, by which means it obtains free egress, and the possibility of a smoky chimney entirely prevented. The scantling of the various timbers, &c., with the exception of the roof, may be the same as those already described; those for the roof, being differently applied, may be of somewhat less dimensions.

The interior of this building should be fitted up in character with the external elevation; but, as the style is plain, and few or no mouldings required, plain champhers and hollows being the characteristics of such buildings, it is presumed, that with the accompanying sheet of details, the builder will be enabled to carry this, as well as the preceding elevations, into execution without any difficulty.

To finish these designs, in a complete and workmanlike manner, will require the following sums, viz.—Elevation, figure 1, £1135; Elevation, figure 2, £985; Elevation, figure 3, £960.

Plate VI.

REFERENCE SHEET OF DETAILS.

Details to Plate IV.

Figure 1.—Perspective sketch of the Ionic capital for elevation.

,, 2.—Base of ditto.

,, 3.—Principal cornice of elevations, Fig. 1 and 3.

,, 4.—Frieze, fillet, and architrave for ditto.

,, 5.—Elevation of truss for Venetian windows.

,, 6.—Side elevation of ditto.

,, 7.—Cap of antea.

,, 8.—Architrave round windows.

,, 9.—Stone-work for balcony of windows to elevation. Fig. 1.

,, 10.—Section of rail for ditto.

,, 11.—Cap of pilaster to same elevation.

,, 12.—Base to ditto.

,, 13.—Cornice for back parlour.

,, 14.—Cornice for front ditto.

,, 15.—Principal bed-room cornice.

,, 16.—Secondary ditto.

Details to Elevation, Figure 4, Plate V.

Figure 17.—Stone coping.

,, 18.—Head of windows.

,, 19.—Mullion of ditto.

,, 20.—Sill of the same.

,, 21.—Elevation of chimney-pot or stone-turret.

,, 22.—Plan of ditto, showing iron fly, or smoke ventilator.

,, 23.—A section of stone gutter, cornice, and portion of roof.

A. Cornice. B. Gutter. C. Wall-plate. D. Rafter. E. Ceiling joists. F. Brick-work. G. Plaster and cornice. H. Battins and slates.

Figure 24.—Plan of stone jamb, frame, and door, &c., for principal entrance.

A. Stone jamb. B. Door-frame. C. Door. D. Architrave.

9

The design represented in Plate VII. is a composition of the Italian, and the plain brick building adopted for cheapness in the present day; and in many situations, would be more consistent than a purer style. It is however strongly recommended, in the erection of those edifices in which an intermixture of styles is adopted, to pay particular attention to the accordance which actually subsists between them; for nothing imparts a more grotesque or unseemly appearance to a building than the introduction of two styles, which do not harmonize with each other; and in all cases it is a certain indication of a vitiated taste, and a direct departure from the genuine principles of architectural beauty.

With a proper view to economy, the walls are intended to be built with bricks, and the embellishments to be finished with Roman cement: the contrast between them will produce a pleasing and imposing effect, provided the bricks be judiciously selected. If the edifice be erected in a county where a plentiful supply of stone can be procured, the use of it would be preferable to that of cement, in consequence of its greater durability, and its decided superiority over every material professing to be an imitation of it. On the same principle cement is preferable to brick, as it possesses a beauty and elegance which can never be attained by the latter material, however excellent the quality may be. A villa built with brick alone, has a mean and secondary appearance; nor even in point of economy is it to be recommended, for as the bricks so used must be of the first class in point of durability and colour, the difference in the expense between their use and that of cement, would in general preponderate in favour of the latter. It must, however, be taken into consideration, that in the adoption of cement, a very scrupulous attention ought to be paid to its selection, for that which is not properly calcined, nor kept perfectly free from the action of the atmosphere after being ground, loses the greater portion of its virtue. Hoping to check the fraud so commonly practised of substituting a spurious article for one that is genuine, and of thus obviating the disappointment which must necessarily occur, we recommend the adoption of the following process as a means of testing the goodness of the article. Take a handful of the cement, and mix it with water to a proper consistency: if caloric be generated, and the mass harden in about five or eight minutes, it may be considered good and suitable for the intended purpose. It may indeed be advanced as an objection by the workman, that the time above-mentioned is too quick to allow of the proper working of the cement; but he must take into his consideration that the mixture of the sand, and the necessary exposure to the atmosphere, will greatly diminish that quickness, and allow a sufficient time for its proper working. In respect to the mixing of lime for laying bricks or for plastering, much must necessarily depend upon its strength, which is increased or diminished according to the quantity of sand that is mixed with it; nor is the quality of the sand a matter of trifling consideration: the pulverized gravel of the horse-roads is preferable to any other that can be selected. The lime itself differs also so much, according to the place from which it is brought, that no specific rules can be laid down for its selection. It will be judicious, therefore, to leave the purchase of it to those who are competent judges of its properties.

Plate VII.

Figure 1. Is a perspective view of the design, exhibiting the end and principal elevation, with a portico: the building may be executed with any suitable material, as before described. Over the end elevation there are four windows, two of which are blank, as well as the four on the upper story. In order to give the building a light appearance, these blank windows should have frames and glazed sashes.

Figure 2. Is the ground floor, consisting of a dining-room, 15 feet by 12 feet; drawing-room, of the same dimensions; porch, 10 feet by 5 feet; passage, 12 feet by 6 feet; staircase, of the same dimensions; kitchen, 14 feet by 12 feet; library, same size; back kitchen, 10 feet 6 inches by 8 feet; conservatory, 8 feet by 7 feet; larder, 6 feet by 5 feet; and water closet, 5 feet by 4 feet. The height of this story is intended to be 10 feet, and to be sound-boarded, and pugged between the floor-joists, which are to be 9 by $2\frac{1}{4}$, properly fixed to the wall-plates according to the method before described.

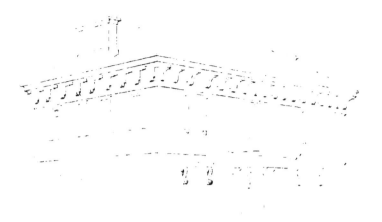

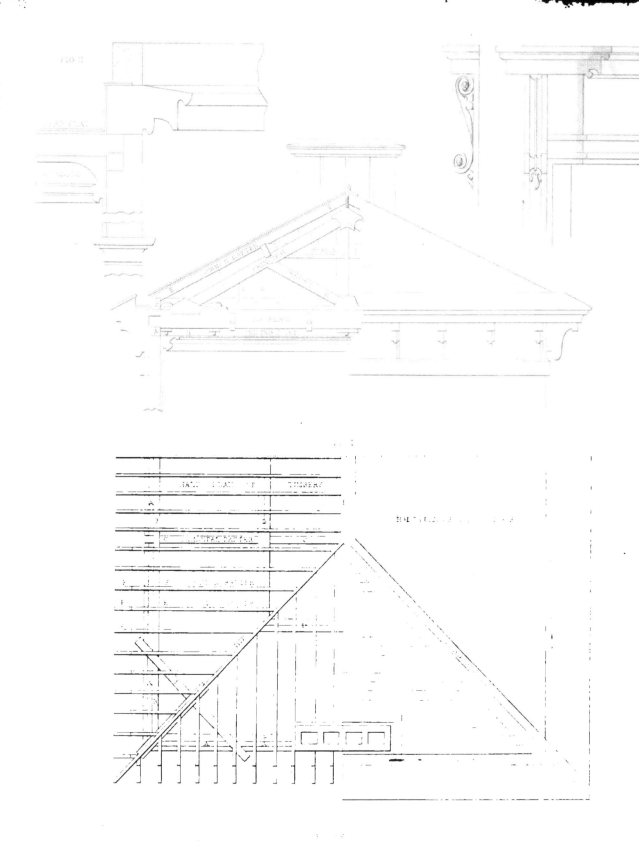

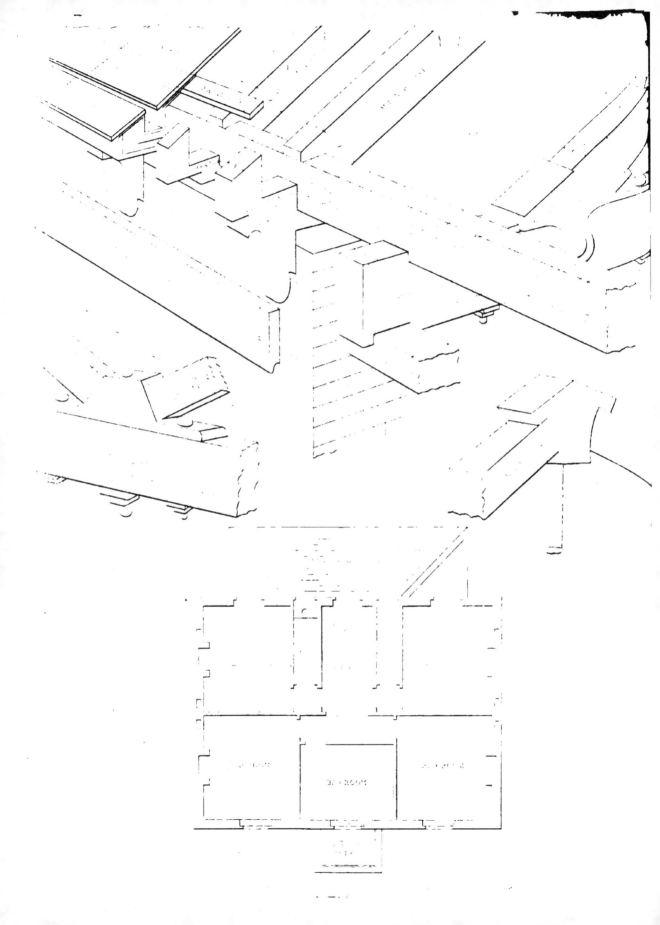

D·E·T·A·I·L·S.

Plate VIII.

Figure 1.—A plan and section of the roof drawn to a scale of one inch and three-quarters to 10 feet, one half of which shows the timber, and the other the finishings.

A. Wall-plate.   B. Pole-plate.   C. Principal rafters.   D. Purlins. E. Common rafters.   F. Bracket and gutter-bearers.   G. Binders, framed into tie-beam.   H. Ceiling-joists.   I. Angle tie.   J. Ridge board. K. Strutts.

Figure 2.—A section of the cornice, antæ, &c. of entrance porch.

Figure 3.—Elevation of principal stone window, dressings, &c.

Figure 4.—Side elevation of truss for the same.

Plate IX.

Is the chamber plan, consisting of a series of five bed-rooms, water-closet, and small store-room, 9 feet in height; the two principal front bed-rooms being 13 feet by 12 feet; the other 12 feet by 9 feet; two back bed-rooms, 13 feet by 12 feet; staircase 13 by 6 feet, with a water-closet and store-closet on each side.   On the top of this Plate are shown the details of the various portions of the roof, exhibiting a gutter formed in the eaves, without in any degree interfering with external appearances; this form should be introduced wherever there is the slightest approach made to the appearance of Italian architecture. A reference will be found to these details in the explanation given in that part of the work appropriated particularly to that subject; it may not, however, be considered improper here to observe, that the construction of the principal rafters is the same as that which has been long established, but the method of receiving the abutments into iron shoes, and confining the whole by an iron rod, is of recent invention, a design which originated from the circumstance of enriched and elaborate ceilings failing or cracking by the shrinking of the principal timbers to which they were attached.   If the cast metal shoes, bolts, &c. be cast according to the calculated pressure or force which they have to resist, it will be found that the ultimate expense will not be greater than that attending the usual way of construction, and the probability of a broken ceiling, cornice, &c. entirely removed.

DETAILS.

Plate IX.

Figure 2.—Head and bolt of cast metal king to principal rafters. The substance of this bolt should be an inch and a half in diameter: a less dimension would be sufficient, if the purity of the metal could be depended upon; but in the construction of buildings it is better to be rather too strong than too weak.

Figure 4.—Cast metal shoe for bottom of the same. These shoes should be cast with the best and softest metal, and as true as possible to the inclination and abutments of the strutts; if properly cast, a substance of three-eighths of an inch round the abutments, as well as the bed upon the tie beam, will be sufficient.

Figure 5.—A sketch to a larger scale of a portion of the roof, showing the construction of the eaves, gutter, &c. This construction has been executed, and found to answer extremely well. It must be perceived that the application is founded upon good principles, inasmuch as every bracket acts as a cantileaver against the front, and under the pole-plate, each of which comes down alternately to the string course, and forms the consols under the eaves.

A. Brick wall. B. Stone string course. C. Bracket and gutter bearer. D. Alternate gutter bearer without bracket. E. Pole-plate. F. Common rafter. G. Batten. H. Slates. I. Tie beam. J. Principal rafter. K. Iron shoe for receiving the foot of ditto.

This building according to the drawing, and the description thus given, may be completed for the sum of about £775.

The cottage represented in Plate X. may be said to belong to the olden style of English architecture, at a period when it began to be enriched by foreign models, and those excrescences were removed, by which, in earlier periods, it was so unfavourably distinguished. A uniformity of design was at one time the acknowledged characteristic of English architecture, when science had very little share in the erection of our private edifices, particularly those of a humbler class; and durability was chiefly regarded, whilst comfort and utility were frequently neglected.

In the accompanying design, it has been the object of the architect to combine economy and comfort with utility and convenience, at the same time that the elegance of the external appearance has not been overlooked. It will be found to be peculiarly adapted for a suburban situation, where the surrounding scenery may be generally said to be more in unison with a chaste and simple style of architecture, than with one which is elaborate or massive. It is, however, an inattention to the existing localities of the intended edifice, that constitutes one of the most serious drawbacks to that exterior harmony and consistency which should characterise our modern edifices, independently of that incongruous mixture of styles, which a perverted taste, combined with ignorance of the most common principles of architectural science, has introduced into the majority of our suburban villas. If erected in the middle of a lawn, the edifice will have a very picturesque appearance.

This cottage is constructed in a similar style of architecture to the design represented in Plate I., and the workmanship is so nearly of the same description, that the sheet of details, Plate III. may be referred to for the erection of this edifice. In the execution of the design it is intended to have a basement story, consisting of a kitchen, 14 feet by 12 feet; scullery, 9 feet by 7 feet; larder, of the same dimensions; servants' room, 14 feet by 12 feet; with staircase, water-closet, &c. This story should be 8 feet 6 inches high, and built, to within 6 inches of the ground-line, with bricks, flints, or stone, according to the produce of the place where it is intended to erect it. If built with bricks, flints, or iron-stone, the plinth should be stuccoed with Roman cement, for receiving the wood sill of the other portion of the superstructure. The first consideration which ought to be given to the basement story is the drainage, which in all buildings is of the greatest importance, not only for the dryness of the habitation, but also for the prevention of any unpleasant effluvia that might arise, from the imperfect method in which drains are generally executed; which will be fully explained in a subsequent part of this work, together with a new method of construction. After the drains are laid and perfect, it would be advisable to fill in to the depth of 12 or 15 inches, with dry lime rubbish, upon which may be laid stone, brick, or asphalte, either of which materials will form a dry floor for the basement. Particular care should be taken, at the same time, to give a proper descent to the various sinks, which should be in immediate communication with the drains. The internal finishings of this floor are intended to be as plain as possible, and consequently require no explanation.

The ground plan consists of a dining-room, 15 feet by 12; drawing-room of the same dimensions; library, 13 feet by 11; hall and staircase of the same dimensions. The dining and drawing-rooms are, in a small degree, increased in size by the bay windows, which, in an erection of this description, have a pretty and consistent internal and external effect. The scantling of the joists for this floor should lie from front to back, and must be 9 inches by $2\frac{1}{4}$, herring-bone trussed, sound-boarded and pugged, and laid with $1\frac{1}{4}$ yellow deal. The finishings of all the rooms must be consistent with those shown on Plate XI. This story is intended to be 9 feet 6 inches in height.

The chamber plan shows a series of five bed-rooms of the same dimensions as the rooms below. The floor joists to be of the same scantling, and the boards of the same thickness as those described for the ground floor, and to be sound-boarded, pugged, &c.; the finishing should be in the same style, but, if possible, plainer. The roof of this building should be constructed in a similar manner to that described in Plate III., and covered with slates, tiles, lead, zinc, reeds, or straw, either of these materials producing a pleasing and picturesque appearance.

Plate X.

Figure 1.—A perspective view of the design, showing the front elevation, and one end of the building. The ascent to the library window,

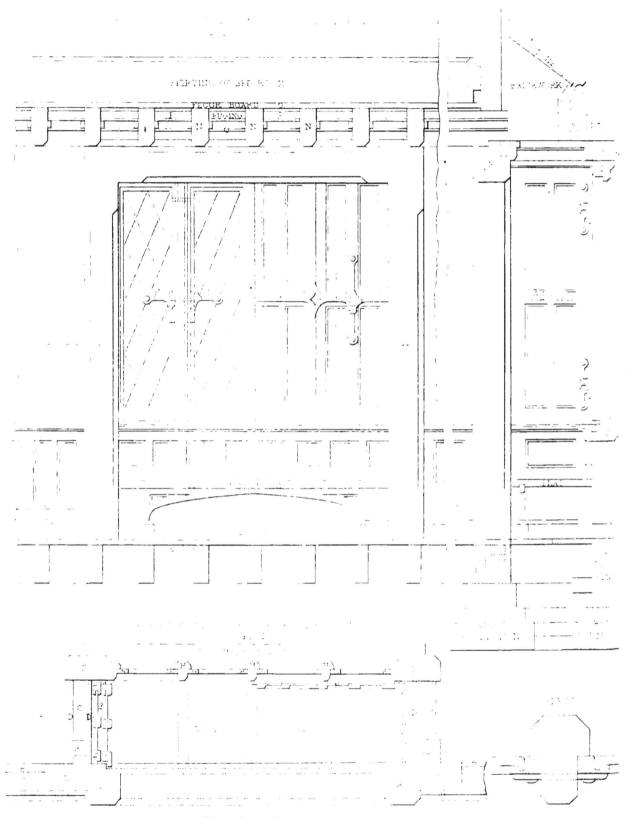

which is a casement, is by means of four steps, over which, from the bed-room, is introduced a characteristic balcony, supported by wood canti-livers, which forms a principal feature in this elevation. The end of this view exhibits the external elevation, &c. of one of the bay windows.

Figure 2.—Elevation of principal front: scale, half an inch to 10 feet.

Figure 3.—Plan of the basement story.

Figure 4.—Plan of ground or principal story.

Figure 5.—Chamber plan.

DETAILS.

Plate XI.

Shows the method of fitting-up one of the bay windows, and fixing the joists of ground and chamber-floors to one of the principal rooms. It will be ob-served in the details given in this plate, that a new casement, with window-head, sill, &c., has been introduced, so formed that it must be as impervious and secure as the most modern sash or French casement; provision being made at the same time for taking off the condensed water, which at all times should be a consideration in rooms where domestic comfort is studied, but which is very frequently entirely omitted, even in buildings of magnitude. A newly-invented spring fastening has also been introduced to these casements, and one for the shutters, which, in consequence of their simplicity, excel any fastening hitherto presented to the public. (See details for casements, shutter and window fastenings, &c.)

Figure 1.—Plan of bay window, one-half of which represents the shutters folded in their boxings, and the other closed, as well as the method of framing the angular posts, wood mullions, &c.

A A. Angular posts. B B. External and internal quarterings. C C. Brick nogging. D D. Plastering. E E. Shutter boxings. F F. Angular stancheons. G. Window sill. H. Mullions.

Figure 2.—Elevation of the same. The letters here employed desig-nate the same parts as on the plan, so far as they correspond; the remainder will refer as follows:—

16

I. Shutters. J. Shutter fastenings. L. Framed back. M. Window-seat. N. Floor joists of chamber story. O. Floor boards. P. Pugging and sound-boarding. Q. Plastering. R. Boards and joists of ground floor.

Figure 3.—A section through the same window, to which the same letters apply, with the following in addition :—

R. Brestsummer. S. Window head. T. Window sill and window head. U. Stone plinth. V. Brick foundation, which, if the basement story be added, must, of course, be taken sufficiently low for that purpose.

Figure 4.—A mullion of the window to a large scale, showing the method of fixing the metal casement to it ; also a wind and water-tight manner of forming the rabbet on the casement.

Plate XII.

Figure 1.—A perspective view of one of the principal rooms, exemplifying the finishing of the ceiling, walls, wainscoting, chimney-piece, &c.

This style of internal finishing has a pleasing and romantic appearance, if properly executed, and in costume with the external portions of the erection. The longitudinal beams of this ceiling are of wood; the small transverse beams are formed in plaster, all of them to be coloured in imitation of oak ; to give relief to the ceiling, the walls are finished in rough stucco, coloured and jointed to imitate stone; the wainscoting may be framed of inch deal, and filleted to form small panels, as described and shown in Plate III. of this work.

The chimney-piece is purposed to be of stone, and might be adopted where an open fire-place is not preferred, which, although more in character with this style of building, has for some years past been dispensed with.

Figure 2.—A plan of the chimney-piece: scale, half an inch to a foot.

Figure 3.—Elevation of the same.

Figure 4.—Capping half full size.

Figure 5.—Bracket and part of shelf, quarter real size.

The other principal rooms on this floor might be fitted up in a similar manner. The hall and stairs should be in keeping with the room described. The chamber floor may be finished quite plain.

This building, according to the drawings, may be finished for the sum of £645.

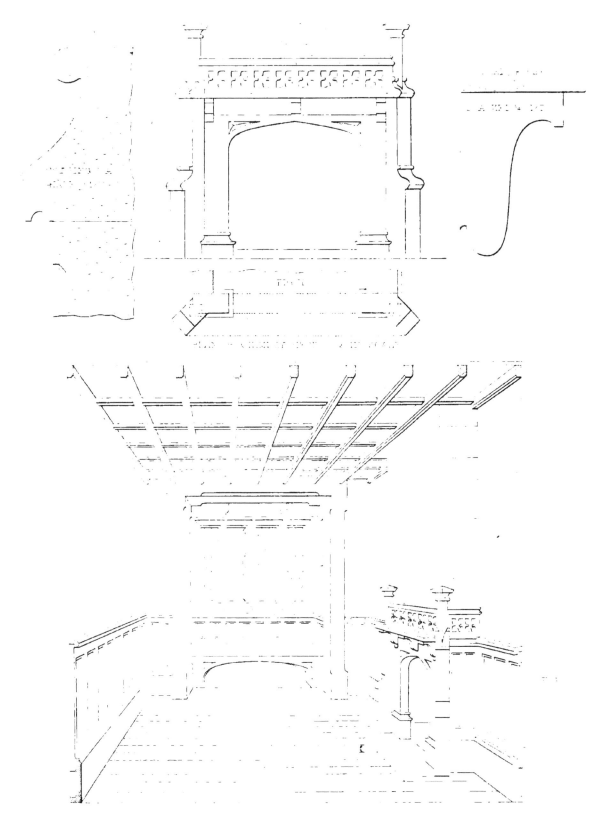

The Venetian style of architecture met with considerable encouragement in this country about the beginning of the eighteenth century; and in many of the edifices of our nobility and gentry, which were erected at that particular period, the principles of that peculiar style are distinctly to be traced.

The progress of a people from a comparative state of barbarism to one of refinement and civilization, particularly in regard to the erection of their edifices, has been generally distinguished by a gradual departure from a complicated and elaborate style to one of greater chasteness and elegance; and the massy and cumbersome edifices of our forefathers, built, as it were, for the duration of ages, are incontestable proofs of a vitiated taste, obtaining the ascendancy over the purer principles of enlightened science. Thus, for instance, in proportion as the taste for architectural beauty and elegance advanced in this country, that extravagant love of exterior ornament and profusion of decoration, which distinguished the earlier ages, gradually subsided, to make room for the introduction of a system founded on a more just conception of the actual principles in which the beauty of an edifice consists, and which are the slow, but certain results of an undeviating attention to the strict and indispensable rules of practical science. When the Venetian style of architecture was in vogue in this country, the taste of the then existing architects was by no means in conformity with those principles which have since been established as the standard and criteria of professional skill. By degrees, however, it became manifest that there were many extravagances in the Venetian style, which detracted considerably from the elegance of the edifice; and by no means could those defects be more successfully remedied than by an intermixture of some of the more classical principles of the Italian style, which possesses in itself many beauties, which are not to be found in the Venetian, and which are highly worthy of being introduced into the architecture of our sub-urban villas. The exterior grandeur and magnificence of the Venetian style, combined with its profusion of extenal ornament, may be in themselves strong recommendations in the erection of a mansion of considerable extent; but in one of more contracted dimensions, where comfort and convenience are the principal objects, combined with simplicity and elegance, the

Italian style, on account of the absence of all redundancy of ornament, is of all others to be preferred.

Thus, plate No. XIII. exhibits a composition of the Italian and Venetian styles of architecture, in which, by their skilful combination, a perspective appearance is obtained, which is highly pleasing and picturesque. It may also be considered as being far more suitable for edifices of a limited extent, than even a more classical or purer style,. in which grandeur and magnificence are generally the leading principles; whereas, in the present design the object which is obtained is elegance in its simple and most pleasing application, without in the least offending the more scrupulous and fastidious eye of the professed architect. This also displays the principal elevation, and ground plan, comprising a small tower, which adds greatly to the effect of the design, without considerably increasing the expense of the erection; and which, in a picturesque country, possesses the advantage of a fine and elevated prospect: this tower is eight feet square internally, and communicates with a - waiting-room, 17 feet by 9; an entrance-hall, 12 feet by 13 feet; sitting-room, 16 feet by 15 feet; library, 15 feet by 13 feet; drawing-room, 16 feet by 15 feet; with suitable staircase, water-closet, &c. It is intended to build the walls with bricks, and to stucco the outside with Roman cement, using stone only, where it becomes necessary. The walls of the highest portions of the building should be carried up two bricks or 18 inches thick; those for the lowest or minor parts, may be one-and-a-half brick, or 14 inches thick; the foundation for the superstructure depends upon the nature of the strata of the soil where it is intended to be erected, which, if it be damp or earthy, should be concreted; the best method of mixing, and applying it for its intended purpose, has been explained in a former part of this work. In a building of this description, and from its irregular height, not producing an equal pressure on the surface of the earth, it is necessary to insert above the footings, and below the floor-joists, a chain-bond, which, in small isolated buildings might be of oak, properly scarfed and framed together. In buildings of larger magnitude, stone bond, properly jointed together, is preferable. The

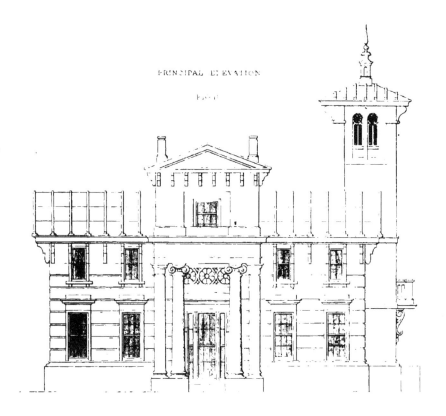

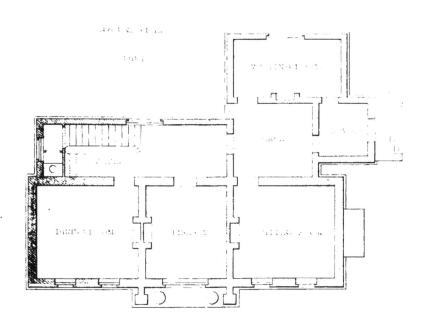

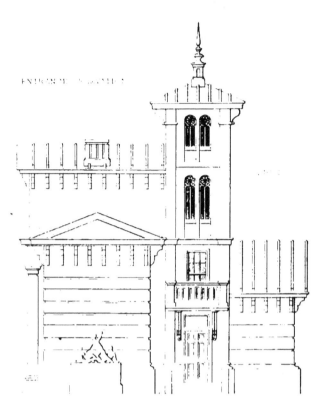

ENDOR SEAT COTTAGE

PLAN OF ONE FLOOR

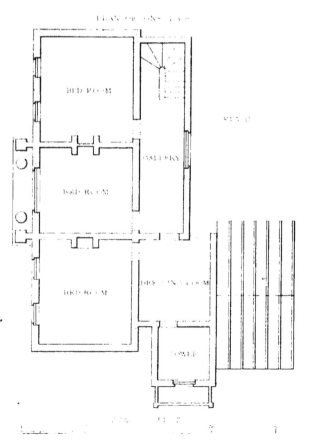

BED ROOM

BED ROOM

BED ROOM

GALLERY

DRESSING ROOM

TOWER

object of either of these bonds being to equalize the pressure or weight upon the earth, as well as to secure firmly all the walls together, every attention should be paid to the proper bedding, as well as the manner of securing the joints. The most approved methods are fully explained in some of the succeeding pages. The joists for this floor should be bedded on sleepers, placed at about four or five feet apart, that in case of any dampness arising from the soil to injure the sleepers or joists, they may be removed, without, in the slightest degree, interfering with the superstructure.

Ventilation should at all times be given between the joists of the various floors, as it dispels dampness; at the same time, particular care should be taken to prevent a draught of air propelling itself into the apartments in too powerful a manner: to prevent which it is desirable to pug between the joists, at the same time allowing sufficient air for the rooms, by ventilators introduced behind the skirting. The height of this floor should be 9 feet 6 inches, the external walls battened, and the finishing suitable to the style of building. Marble chimney-pieces for these rooms become indispensable; which may be introduced, since the adoption of machinery to the working and polishing of marble, has reduced its price nearly 20 per cent. A visit to the Marble Company's Works, situate in Esher Street, Holywell Street, Westminster, will not only prove the accuracy of this statement, but exemplify the superiority of the machinery for polishing, over manual labour.

Figure 1.—Plate XIV. shows the end or entrance elevation.

Figure 2.—The plan of chamber-story, of three good-sized and suitable bed-rooms, and a corresponding dressing-room. The height of this story should be 9 feet; the joists, 9 inches by $2\frac{1}{4}$ inches; sound-boarded, pugged, and trussed; and covered with $1\frac{1}{4}$ inch yellow deal floor boards.

20

Plate XV.

REFERENCE TO DETAILS.

Exemplifies the construction of a wrought metal roof, and if properly applied is cheaper and lighter than the old method of framing wood roofs. In this sheet, a wood wall plate and wood binding joists are shown; but where a plastered ceiling is dispensed with, as would be the case in many instances, a stone wall plate is recommended. The first roof, executed of this description was at the Retort House of the Gas Works, at Leek, in Staffordshire, which was found to be much cheaper than wood, and answer every anticipated purpose. The external appearance, can however, be considerably improved, by covering the roof with a patent slating, invented by a gentleman of the name of North, who has an extensive slate-yard in the New Palace Road, Lambeth. These slates are generally about half an inch thick, 5 feet long, and 3 feet or 3 feet 6 inches wide, and fixed on the roof as shown in the plate. A slate gutter and bearers are also introduced, which, by being properly applied and cemented, will have a light and beautiful effect. It will be obvious by inspecting the diagram, Fig. 3, that the slates have an inclination to a chasm formed in the joint, by which means the water falls into the trench which the wood roll covers, and thereby prevents the water over shooting the front portion of the gutter. This method of guttering and roofing, may be adopted with as little expense as the old established system, and the security of the building generally, as well as the external beauty, be considerably improved; independently of possessing the advantage of having no visible gutter.

Figure 1.—A. Brick wall. B. Slate bearers. C. Slate Gutters. D. North's patent slates. E. Wood roll. F. Metal rafter. G. Wall plate. H. Metal tie beam. I. Wood binder.

Figure 2.—A section quarter real size, showing the method of securing the patent slates to the purlins, &c.

Figure 3.—A geometrical section, one quarter real size of wood roll, slates, and principal rafter.

This building may be executed for about the sum of £925.

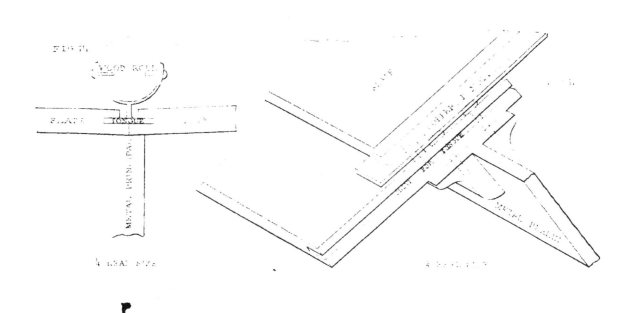

of it a new, national, and consistent style of building. If these principles be admitted, that nation has undoubtedly the merit of a particular style of architecture, whose edifices correspond, in the first place, with the climate, with the style of construction adapted to the materials, and with the sentiments and manners of the nation and of the times; and secondly, which constitute in their principal forms, and in their several parts and ornaments, a whole in harmony with itself, excluding or rejecting every thing that is foreign or unsuitable.

A building may be well arranged for all the purposes of mere convenience, but in this case it is not an architectural construction. The progress which the arts have made in modern times has taught us to combine internal convenience and fitness with beauty of external form, and with durability. If the external arrangement of a building should be compounded of those of several nations, such as Hindoo, Egyptian, and Grecian, we should not admit this to be an architectural construction, even if the external form were an object of pleasure, which, however, is hardly a possible result; for it is essential to the character of an architectural structure, that the general arrangement and ornaments should exhibit a unity of character, and be referable to some particular period.

The design represented in Plate XVI. may be considered a combination of the Grecian and the Italian styles; and perhaps there are not any two, when skilfully and scientifically combined, which present a more pleasing appearance. The elegant simplicity of the former accords well with the more florid and elaborate style of the latter; and where the primitive characters of both are strictly maintained, and their respective beauties judiciously introduced, without the slightest admixture of those incongruous subjects which are too often displayed in our modern edifices, the style, as exhibited in the accompanying design, may be strongly recommended as the one most proper to be adopted in the erection of our suburban villas; possessing at the same time the important advantage that the expense attending the erection is comparatively small, when calculated in reference to edifices of greater magnitude.

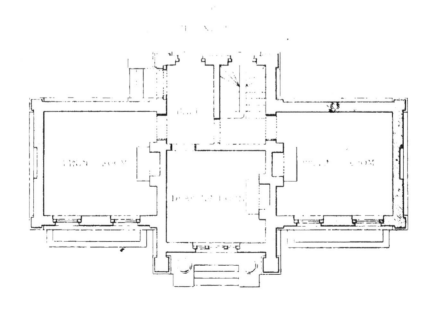

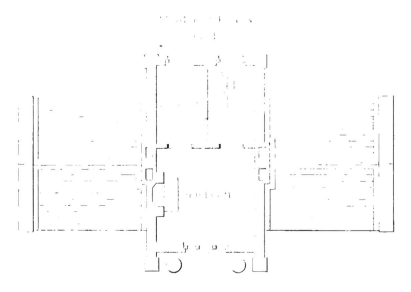

23

The walls of this building should be 18 inches thick, to the floor line; the principal or centre portion may then be carried up 1½ bricks or 14 inches, and the wings 9 inches; the whole is intended to be stuccoed in imitation of stone, with Roman cement, which if properly executed, strengthens the brick work equal to half a brick added in thickness. The joists for the ground floor should be 6 inches by 2 inches, properly and securely bridged to oak sleepers, bedded upon brick piers.

Plate XVI.

Figure 1. Exhibits the principal or ground plan, consisting of a hall, 9 feet by 6; dining-room, 16 feet by 12; sitting-room of the same dimensions; with a drawing-room 12 feet by 11. It will be perceived that the entrance to this building is on the opposite side to the principal rooms, thereby exposing the façade to a lawn, or pleasure grounds.

Figure 2. Shows the geometrical elevation of the building: the dotted lines below the ground line indicate the depth to which it is purposed to take the basement story, where the kitchen and other servants' offices may be placed, the dimensions of which must of course, if carried into execution in this way, be arranged according to the rooms above.

Plate XVII.

Figure 1. Shows the arrangement of the first floor or bed-room story. This floor should have joists, 9 inches by 2 inches, resting on the flank-walls, securely fixed to wall-plates 4½ by 3 inches; trimmers 9 by 3. The span of the roofs being small, no principal rafters will be required, couples framed in the usual way being quite sufficient. The wall-plate should be $4\frac{1}{2}$ by $3\frac{1}{2}$, couples or collar rafters 6 inches by 3, common rafters 3 inches by 2 inches, purlins 4 by $2\frac{1}{2}$. The scantling of the other timbers must correspond.

Figure 2.—A perspective sketch of the Venetian window of principal front.

Figure 3.—One of the consoles to a large scale.

Figure 4. Shows the cornice and one of the ornaments to a similar scale.

Plate XVIII.

Figure 1.—A sketch of the principal cornice, showing the method of bedding the stone core for receiving the stucco, &c.

Figure 2.—A sketch of the antæ.

Figure 3.—A section of the cornice of drawing-room.

Figure 4.—Plan of the same.

Figure 5.—Shows the ground jamb linings, a portion of the door stile, and mouldings of two different architraves.

Figure 6.—Presents a design of a chimney-piece in the same style of architecture, for the drawing-room.

Figure 7.—Is a sketch of one of the consoles of the same.

Figure 8.—The ground plan of the chimney-piece.

Figure 9.—A method of finishing the external appearance of the chimneys.

This building, according to the description and drawings, may be executed for about the sum of £560.

In delineating the plan or design of the different kinds of edifices, whether intended immediately for ornament or absolute utility, there is an admitted scope for an almost infinite variety, according to the peculiar taste of the architect, or to the prevailing fashion of the age in which he lives, or to the situation, object, or extent of the edifice which it is designed to erect. It must, however, be acknowledged that every architect, like the painter or the poet, is more or less a mannerist, and that in the majority of cases, a building has only to be examined in its principal details, to arrive at once at the knowledge of the individual who was the architect of it; on the same principle that the connoisseur has only to inspect a picture, to determine at once upon the studio from which it emanated. The foregoing remark may be forcibly illustrated, by an examination of the edifices designed by different architects, for it will be found that each one has a style peculiar to himself. In all the designs that have been made for the present work, we have endeavoured so to introduce a judicious mixture of the most approved and elegant styles of architecture, that, without offending any of the acknowledged rules of architectural science, and at the same time, carefully avoiding those incongruities and inconsistencies which an ill-regulated intermixture of styles is in general too apt to produce, such an edifice may be presented to the intending builder, as is not only elegant and ornamental, but chaste and tasteful in all its relations and proportions.

In the beginning of the seventeenth century, the models of· the Grecian and Roman styles of architecture were closely followed in the erection of the public buildings of this country, and they have, without any material deviation, been adhered to, up to the present time. In attempting, however, to reduce the plans of our modern edifices, designed principally for the purposes of common life, to the standard of the Grecian and Roman school, a considerable degree of difficulty and inconvenience was found perpetually to arise; to remedy which, recourse was had to all the extravagancies of an exuberant imagination, which would not deign to be fettered by any of the rules which science or experience had laid down as the standard of a genuine and refined taste; and to this circumstance may very properly be attributed many of those deformities and absurdities for which several of the principal edifices of the present day are distinguished. It is not, however, hereby meant to infer, that in the composition of architectural designs, no appeal whatever is to be made to the exercise of fancy; but on the contrary, that the architect should be bound down to a set of formal rules, which being founded on the acknowledged principles of science, are to be held as sacred, and never to be departed from, however much the beauty or elegance of the design may require it. It must, however, be confessed, that it is in the violation of those rules, that the judgment and discrimination of the architect are frequently the most conspicuously displayed: the very extent and power of his genius are manifested in the skill which he evinces in the adaptation of the several parts of his edifice to their respective uses and places, so that the whole may exhibit a just and correct correspondence in all its various details, and such a tasteful combination be produced, as declares at once the hand and mind of the master, without which no edifice can be said to be complete.

In the accompanying design (Plate XIX.) formed on the model of the Grecian style of architecture, it is confidently presumed, that the principles just advanced will be acknowledged to have been carried properly into execution; at the same time that a faithful adherence has been paid to those fixed and established rules, in which the beauty and excellence of all edifices may be said to consist.

Plate XIX.

Shows a ground plan and perspective sketch. This design may be classed above the scale of buildings which have hitherto been introduced in this work, and may with propriety be designated as an erection forming an intermediate chain between the cottage and the villa.

Figure 1.—The ground floor, consisting of a hall, lobby, breakfast-room, drawing-room, library, dining-room, water-closet, kitchen, scullery, store-room, stairs, &c.

FIG. 1
GROUND PLAN

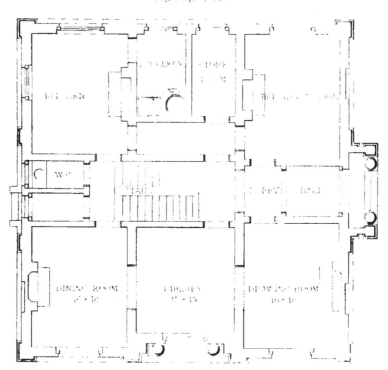

SCALE OF FEET

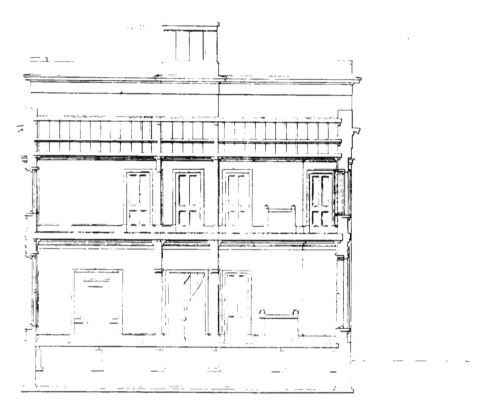

SECTION TAKEN ON LINE A-B

FIRST FLOOR PLAN

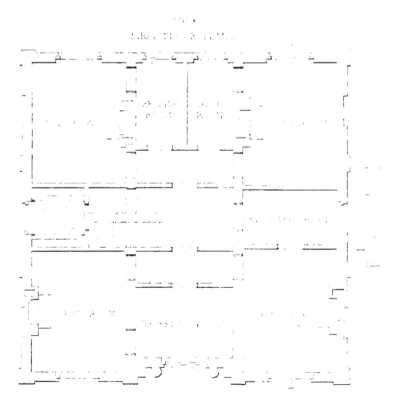

SCALE OF FEET

Figure 2. Is a perspective sketch of the building, the nearest angle of which, by applying to the scale, will give the requisite proportions.

The terrace, &c. are matters of secondary consideration, and the building is complete without them; but in a situation where the surrounding scenery is consistent, they are embellishments which should not be dispensed with.

Plate XX.

A section and plan of the same.

Figure 1.—The plan, consisting of four bed-rooms and four dressing-rooms, which may occasionally be converted into small bed-rooms.

Figure 2. Presents a section taken through the principal rooms, which it is presumed the mechanic who performs the building department, will easily understand. The line A B, marked on the plan, shows the position in which the section is taken.

D E T A I L S.

Plate XXI.

Introduces a sheet of details to the preceding design, which exemplifies a new method of suspending the doors communicating with the principal rooms, &c.

Figure 1.—A section of the door, one-half of which shows it shut, and the other in its casing.

Figure 2.—Half elevation of door, as it would appear when closed.

Figure 3.—Half the longitudinal section of the same, supposing one side of the partition to be taken away.

A. Door. B. Iron suspension bar. C C. Wheels. D D. Shows the method of fixing the same to the doors. E E. The chair, and manner of fixing it, for receiving the iron suspension bar, to the upright quartering of partition. *a*. Upright quartering. *c c*. Bolts for securing the chops of wheels to doors, &c. *d d*. Side rollers to receive the door, as it moves by the springs which are fixed in the internal casing; by applying the thumb to a small spring behind the architrave, the doors will open and shut at pleasure. *e e*. Springs, &c.

Figure 4.—Section of the door.

Figure 5.—A perspective sketch of the doors suspended.

A. Quartering. B. Chair for receiving the iron suspension bar. C. Iron suspension bar. D D. Wheel and chops for fixing the door and wheel together to the door sill.

Figure 6.—Section of door panel. The following figures are one-eighth the real size.

Figure 7.—Elevation of the same.

Figure 8.—Skirting of room.

Figure 9.—Section of architrave, door, &c. with iron suspension attached.

Figure 10.—Elevation of the same.

This building, according to the drawings and the description, may be completed for about the sum of £1300.

29

Architecture, when considered in its chief and most important relations, may be divided into two prominent and distinguishing characters, namely, the useful and the ornamental; and it may be considered as having approached its acmé of perfection, when both are so intimately blended, that neither carries away the superiority, whilst at the same time the end in view has been satisfactorily and advantageously attained. Buildings in general may be divided into three kinds: 1st, those which are intended solely for use; 2nd, those which are directly ornamental; and, 3rd, those which exhibit a combination of both. In regard to the former, they ought in every part and particular to correspond with the intent in view, and the slightest deviation from that correspondence, even though it should approximate to the ornamental, possesses a disagreeable and incongruous character; for as every edifice adapted solely for use, can be regarded only as the mean for the attainment of some particular end, it follows of course that the principal circumstance to be attended to in the erection of an edifice is, in what manner that mean can be brought to the highest state of perfection, in the attainment of which even beauty itself, when it appears in opposition to it, must be discarded as improper and inconsistent. On the other hand, those edifices which are intended merely as ornamental, such as columns, obelisks, triumphal arches, &c., beauty and ornament alone ought to be consulted; in illustration of which we may refer to the triumphal arch at Hyde Park Corner, or the obelisk surmounted by the statue of the Duke of York, with the erection of which not the slightest utility was combined, and consequently architectural beauty was the sole aim and study of the architect; and in the greater or less attainment of that property may be said to consist the comparative degree of his skill and science. In all architectural buildings, however, the chief difficulty which presents itself is the just combination of the useful with the ornamental; and in order to accomplish that much-desired end, different and even opposite means must be frequently resorted to, which is in itself one of the principal reasons why they are so seldom united so as to produce a positive degree of perfection.

In all buildings intended solely or chiefly to please the eye, architectural

K

regularity and proportion are essentially necessary, because from their combination may be said to emanate the real intrinsic beauty of an edifice; but on the other hand, an architect ought not to confine his attention solely to regularity and proportion, necessary as they may be, but he must also study congruity, which is always observable when the form and ornament of a structure are properly adapted to the purposes for which it is intended; the result of which is, that every building ought to exhibit that peculiar style which is indicative of the particular uses for which it is erected.

In the majority of cases, the Gothic style of architecture for modern designs is to be preferred to the more classical, although a selection of that kind may seem to be attended with a considerable degree of difficulty. It must, however, be borne in mind that the true style or character applicable to edifices of this description, may properly be designated as the ancient English style of building, but now more generally known by the epithet of Gothic; and is particularly to be recommended for those edifices in which a rural or rustic appearance is intended to be produced; at the same time it must be observed that the high pointed arches, pinnacles, enriched tracing work, and the other distinguishing features of the florid and church Gothic, are wholly inapplicable to edifices of a private character, and should be utterly discarded as indicative of a vitiated taste.

A reference to Plate XXII. will illustrate the truth of the foregoing remarks, it being a design for a shooting-box on a limited scale, in which an attempt is made, and it is to be hoped a successful one, to combine utility with ornament, and at the same time possessing all those conveniences, which are indispensable in an edifice of this kind. It is in erections of this character, that the skill of the architect is principally displayed, as, not being confined to any peculiar style, he may give a more enlarged scope to the suggestions of his taste, and make use of those ornaments with greater license and profusion which are not generally admissible in a really classical edifice.

Plate XXII. exhibits the principal elevation and ground plan, consisting

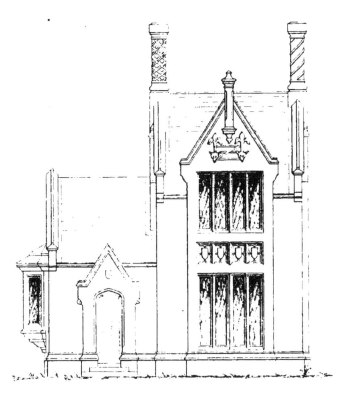

PRINCIPAL ELEVATION

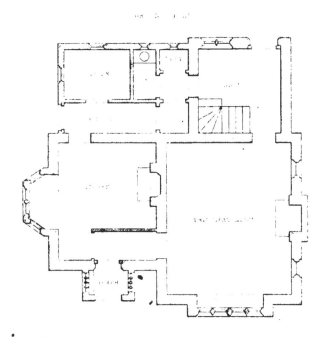

of an entrance porch, 7 feet by 4, communicating with a passage 8 feet by 4, leading to the principal room, 18 feet by 14 feet, with ingress to the hall and stairs, 10 feet square, with suitable larder, water-closet, convenience for coals and dust, passage, &c.

The principal room and hall of this floor should be 10 feet in height from the flooring to the ceiling; the other offices should be 8 feet high; the walls to be built in cement, and the foundation at least 18 inches below the surface, with suitable footings for receiving 14-inch walls for the higher portions of the building, and 9-inch walls for the offices. If the soil be loamy or damp, concrete must be used under the foundation.

The principal room on this floor must be covered with $1\frac{1}{4}$-inch yellow deal boards, properly fixed upon floor joists 6 by $2\frac{1}{2}$, properly bedded on sleepers 4 by 4, fixed upon brick piers at proper distances. Bond timber $4\frac{1}{2}$ by 3, should be inserted every seventh course, properly halved and scarfed and nailed together, as well as securely dove-tailed at the angles, not only as a preventive against dampness, but as imparting an extra strength to the walls, the intended thinness of which renders drainage a matter of the very first consideration, and it is a point which cannot be too strongly recommended in almost every dwelling, however apparently dry may be the situation.

The joiner's work, such as doors, shutters, architraves, &c. should be fitted up as directed in the drawing, and according to the sizes already specified for erections of a similar description. Particular care should be taken to preserve their proper and consistent proportions, otherwise a risk will be run of producing a deformity which will prove a great drawback to the general beauty of the edifice.

The wall plates of the first floor should be 6 inches by 3, properly halved, scarfed, and spiked together, as well as securely dove-tailed at the angles. The joists should be 9 by $2\frac{1}{2}$, and covered with $\frac{1}{4}$-inch yellow deal with straight joints and splayed leadings. The span of this roof being narrow, the principal rafters will not be required, as common rafters will be found sufficient. The size of the other various scantlings must be applied according to the different situations for which they are intended.

Plate XXIII. exhibits the end elevation and plan of the upper floor, containing the principal bed-room, and two servants' bed-rooms over the offices. This elevation when viewed in perspective, will exhibit a beautiful appearance against the horizon, in consequence of its broken outline.

Plate XXIV. shows the method of fitting up the bay windows of the principal room, as exemplifying a new method of action in the shutter, which is moved up and down by springs acting in concert with each other, thereby dispensing with the unsightly appearance of cords, &c. which in a room finished in this style of building, should at all times be avoided.

To complete this building according to the drawings, will require about the sum of 375*l*.

DETAILS OF PLATE XXIV.

Figure 1. Shows the half internal section of the window, before the metal casements are fixed, and exhibiting the spiral spring for the shutters.

Figure 2. Exhibits the internal elevation of the window, with casement fixed, and delineating the architraves. The dotted lines show the position of descending shutters.

Figure 3.—Transverse section of the window, indicating the method of fixing casements, shutters, &c.

Figure 4.—Ground plan of window.

SIDE ELEVATION

FIRST FLOOR PLAN

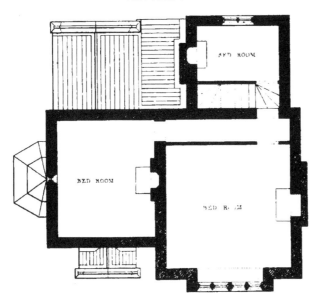

BED ROOM

BED ROOM

BED ROOM

The Grecian style of architecture has long held a distinguished place in the estimation of modern architects, not only on account of the elegance of its general outline, but also for the pleasing combination of the magnificent with the simple, and the grand and sublime with the useful and ornamental. There is something divine in man, which prompts him to look beyond the mere supply of his necessities, and to aim at continually higher objects; he therefore soon expected from his habitations and his temples more than mere utility; he aimed at elegance, and architecture became by degrees a fine art, differing, however, essentially from the other fine arts in two important particulars: first, that it is based on utility; and secondly, that it elevates mathematical laws to rules of beauty. Painting and sculpture are only the expression of the feeling of the beautiful; whilst, on the contrary, every creation of architecture must appear to have utility in view. A column, or an entablature, which supports nothing, appears ridiculous; and every part of the building ought to show the purpose for which it is designed. Architecture appears to have been among the earliest inventions, and its works have been commonly regulated by some principle of hereditary imitation. Whatever rude structure the climate and materials of any country have obliged its early inhabitants to adopt for their temporary shelter, the same structure, with all its prominent features, has been afterwards kept up by their refined and opulent posterity. Thus the Egyptian style of building has its origin in the cavern and mound; the Chinese architecture is modelled from the tent; the Grecian is derived from the wooden cabin; and the Gothic from the bower of trees.

Grecian architecture is considered to have been in its greatest perfection in the age of Pericles and Phidias. The sculpture of this period is admitted to have been superior to that of any other age; and although architecture be a more arbitrary art than sculpture, yet it is natural to conclude, that the state of things which gave birth to the excellence of the one, must have produced a corresponding power of conceiving sublimity and beauty in the other. Tuscan architecture was in general distinguished by simplicity of structure, fewness of parts, absence of arches, lowness of pediments and roofs, and of decorative curves, the outline of which was a spiral line, or conic section, and not a circular arc, as afterwards adopted by the Romans.

In edifices erected at the present day, the Grecian and Gothic outlines are commonly employed to the exclusion of the rest. In choosing between them, the fancy of the builder, more than any positive rules of fitness, must direct the decision. Modern dwelling-houses have necessarily a style of their own, as far as stories, and apartments, and windows, and chimneys can give them one. No more of the styles of former ages can be applied to them, than what may be called the unessential and decorative parts. In general, the Grecian style, from its right angles and straight entablatures, is more convenient, and fits better with the distribution of our common edifices than the pointed and irregular Gothic. The expense is also generally less, especially if any thing like thorough and genuine Gothic be attempted. But the occasional introduction of the Gothic outline, and the partial employment of its ornaments, have undoubtedly an agreeable effect, both on public and private edifices; and we are indebted to it, among other things, for the spire, a structure exclusively Gothic, which, though often misplaced, has become an object of general approbation, and a pleasing land-mark to cities and villages.

The Grecian style of architecture, as exemplified in Plate XXV., can be applied with the most beautiful effect in any elevated situation, as the outline against the horizon, in its general appearance, is both pleasing and elegant. It is, however, desirable in the erection of a building of this kind, as indeed in all others, where the productions of nature are to be brought into unison with the principles of art, that the locality of the situation should be an object of the first consideration; and it is the gross inattention to this fundamental principle, which is the cause of so many incongruities and absurdities, which are so glaringly visible in the erection of our modern villas. An intuitive knowledge of architecture, based on the principles of taste and science, is a direct gift of nature, and hence arises the necessity of an application to men of confirmed professional skill, in order that those defects and incongruities may be avoided, into which the uninitiated architect is so apt to fall.

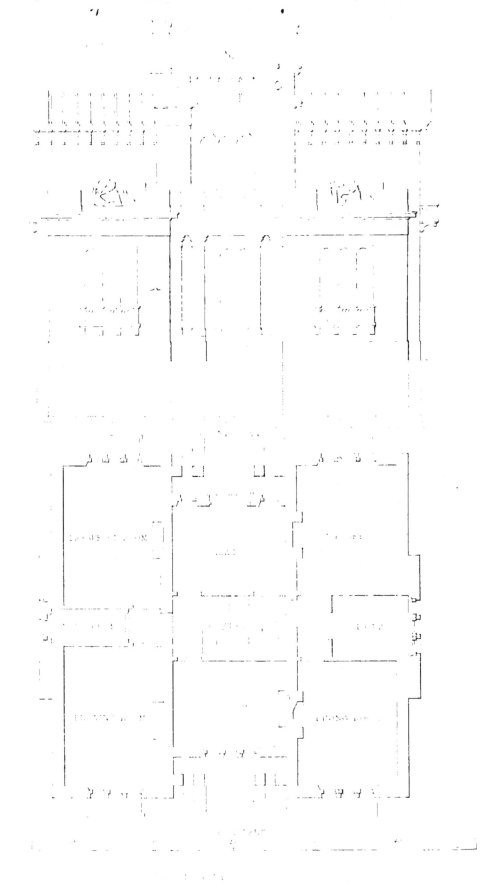

Plate XXV.

Contains the principal elevation and ground plan: the dotted lines on the elevation show where the kitchen and suitable offices may be erected underneath; but if the situation be convenient, they should be built on a contiguous piece of ground, without any excavation, and a portion of the ground under the principal building might be dug out for cellars.

If this plan be carried into execution, the excavated part, or cellaring, may be divided into the after-mentioned apartments, namely, a kitchen 17 feet by 12 feet; a servants' hall of the same dimensions; housekeeper's room, and butler's pantry, of somewhat less dimensions, combined with suitable wine, ale, and beer-cellars, and other requisite conveniences. The kitchen, servants' hall, cellars, &c., should be paved with stone, paving-tiles, or bricks, according to the produce that can be obtained on or about the site of the erection. The drainage, and preparation of the sub-soil, in order to prevent dampness arising, must of course be a matter of important consideration. A system of ventilation should also be introduced, as nothing can possibly be more annoying to persons of delicate olfactory nerves than the effluvia that arise from the culinary department of the offices. In the fitting up and furnishing of the domestic offices, great care should be taken, as the comfort of the entire house much depends upon the arrangements there adopted. Many persons imagine that the method of finishing them is of so slight importance, that if a reduction is to be made in the estimated price of a building, the difficulty is almost always met by the adoption of some inferior method of performing the necessary work in this department of the building. We are, however, of opinion, that if any part of a house should be more carefully finished than another, it should be the kitchens and domestic offices; and the floor above them should always be sound-boarded and pugged. The thickness of the walls, from the basement to the ground-floor, should be at least $2\frac{1}{2}$ bricks, or 1 foot $10\frac{1}{2}$ inches thick. Indeed, it should be regulated according to their various situations, and the weights they have to support. The housekeeper's room and butler's pantry should have floor-joists 4½ by two inches, properly bedded on sleepers, and covered with 1¼ yellow deal floor-boards.

The ground-floor, Figure 2, consists of an entrance hall, which is ascended by five steps, rising 6 inches each from the ground, 14 feet by 11 feet; communicating with a stair-case, 14 feet by 8 feet; a saloon, 14 feet by 11 feet; dining-room, 15 feet by 13 feet; library of the same dimensions; drawing-room, 17 feet by 13 feet; breakfast-room, same size: with a small waiting and still room. The hall-staircase and saloon should be paved with stone, on 4½ inch brick arches, turned over upon metal girders prepared and fixed for that purpose. The joists for the other rooms should be 9 inches by 2¼, properly secured to wall-plates 9 + 6. This floor, of course, should be herring-bone trussed, sound-boarded, pugged, and covered with 1¼ inch yellow deal; straight joint and side nailed, with splayed heading joints. It may be proper to observe, that in placing the various tiers of bond timber that are requisite, they should project at least half an inch before the internal surface of the brick-work; consequently the scantling, to make good work, should be the thickness of a brick, and half an inch wider. This method of placing the bond timber should be only adopted when the walls are battened, and which should be done to all external walls of every habitation, where dampness is considered possible. The climate of this country being so changeable, and the materials generally, whether of stone or brick, very porous, the moisture of the atmosphere is readily absorbed, which, to a certain extent, is introduced into the various apartments by the caloric contained therein; in consequence of which the paper, and other embellishments of the rooms, become defaced and injured. It is evident, therefore, that a chasm of even only half an inch from the internal surface of the brick wall, will, to a great extent, if not entirely, prevent the condensation of a damp or humid atmosphere penetrating into the apartments; and the adoption of this method will certainly be found more beneficial, if all the timber used in the erection be subjected to the ordeal of Kyan's patent method of destroying the fungi which in the generality of timber, cause capillary attraction, engendering what is technically termed dry rot, and effecting the rapid decay of the timber.

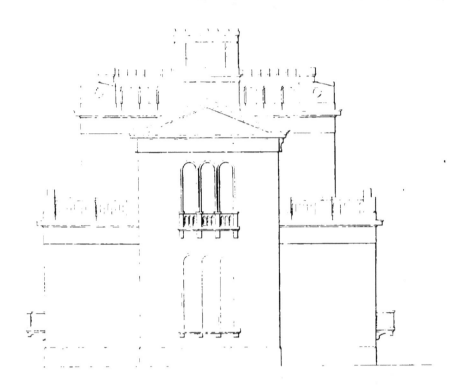

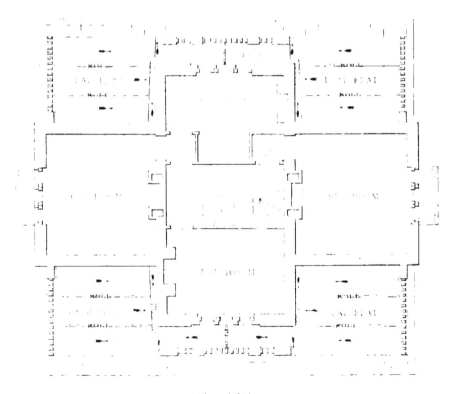

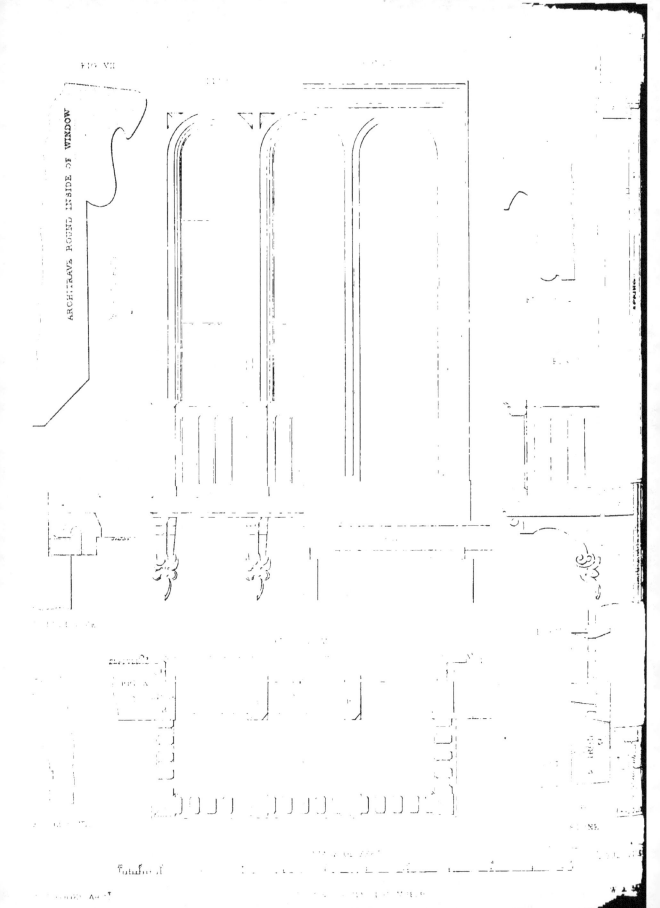

ARCHITRAVE ROUND INSIDE OF WINDOW

Plate XXVI.—End elevation and plan of one-pair floor.

This elevation, in execution may at the first view appear plain and unpleasing, when compared with the preceding one, but when viewed in perspective it will not have that effect, but produce a pleasing breadth of light and shade.

The one-pair floor consists of two bed-rooms, 15 feet by 13 feet; one, 14 feet by 10 feet; and the other, 12 feet by 11 feet; with a plan of the flats, &c. showing the various falls to the gutters, and which might be laid with lead, zinc, or marine metal. This floor should be 9 feet 6 inches high; and constructed with joists, boards, &c. similar to those described for the floor below. The attic story consists of a similar number of bed-rooms, but not so high, and consequently might be applied to the use of the domestics; the roof being of short bearings may be framed in a manner before explained for this style of building, care being taken to preserve its external appearance.

Plate XXVII.

REFERENCE SHEET OF DETAILS.

The details of the principal windows.

This style of window, when introduced in Grecian architecture, has a light and pleasing appearance, and by dispensing with the old and bad method of suspending the sashes by cords attached to weights, not only improves the effect, but renders them more secure and impervious to the weather.

Figure 1.—Plan showing balcony, mullions of windows, cast metal casement, shutters, spring lifts and falls, architraves, &c.

M

A. York landing. B. Mullions and jambs of Bath stone. C. Brick wall. D. Stucco. E. Plaster inside of room. F. Cast-metal casement. G. Balustrades of balcony.

Figure 2.—Outside elevation of same window.

Figure 3.—Inside of ditto; the dotted lines below the sill indicate the panel of sliding shutters, which are intended to act by springs instead of cords and weights, thereby dispensing with the appearance of cords in the fitting up of the principal rooms.

Figure 4.—Section of the same.

A. Stone head. B. Brick work. C. Stucco. D. Spring for shutter. E. Cast-metal casement. F. Stone landing for balcony, which embraces sill of window, &c. G. Cavity for taking off the surface water of the same. H. Profile of cantaliver. I. Stucco. J. Brick work. K. Shutters. L. Floor joist. M. Floor boards. N. Sleepers.

Figure 5.—Section of the bar of cast-metal casement.

Figure 6.—Elucidates a section of the method of the swinging casement closing upon the sill of the same.

A. Bottom rail of opening casement. B. Sill of the same. C. Trough for condensed water which may fall from casement. D. A drill hole in each casement for taking off the same. E. Wood blocking. F. Stone sill. G. A lead plug let into the same, for receiving a screw for securing the wood blocking, which is sunk in, and covered over with the centre-bit plug. H. Hinge for flap that covers sliding shutter.

Figure 7.—Moulding for architrave of Figure 2.

Figure 8.—Moulding for external landing of balcony.

Figure 9. Cap of ditto.

Figure 10. The opening and fixed jamb of cast-metal casement, that is purposed to move on a centre.

Plate XXVIII.

Detail of principal entrance door.

This door is intended to have the appearance of double doors, although framed as a single one. It is purposed to act upon a pivot, which for external uses is at all times preferable to hinges, in consequence of their weight, as producing the means of better security.

Figure 1. Half external elevation.
" 2. Half internal elevation.
" 3. Section of the same
" 4. Plan of ditto.
" 5. Plan of portion of door to a large scale.
" 6. Elevation of one of side lights adjoining door.
" 7. Mouldings of entablature of door to a large scale.
" 8. External architrave.

Plate XXIX.

Shows the details of external mouldings, &c. drawn to one-eighth real size.

Figure 1. Principal cornice, with truss, &c.
" 2. Elevation of truss.
" 3. Cornice round attic.
" 4. Chimney shaft.
" 5. Base of ditto.
" 6. Sill of plain windows.
" 7. Cap of pilasters.
" 8. Cornice to principal rooms. It is purposed to fix the bell enrichment in every angle of the room.
" 9. Cornice of principal bed-rooms.

Figure 10. Exhibits a new method of fixing stone ashlering to the bond stone, whereby the said bond stone can settle with the brick work without injuring the face of the ashlering.

In the construction of buildings, where brick and stone are used for the erection of the walls, stone-work being generally much larger than the bricks, a consequent settlement will take place more in the one than the other, and fractures in the stability of the structure will consequently ensue. To remedy this, the method here exhibited has been found to answer the purpose effectually, by allowing the bond stone to slide with the settlement of the brick-work upon a plug let in for that purpose.

Plate XXX.

Perspective view of the building.

Figure 1. Elevation of design for a chimney-piece of one of the principal rooms.
" 2. Plan of the same.
" 3. Section of ditto.
" 4. Moulding of shelf to a large scale.
" 5. Elevation of chimney-piece for principal bed-rooms.
" 6. Plan of the same.
" 7. Moulding of shelf to a large scale.

To execute this building in a proper and substantial manner will cost about the sum of £1985.

PERSPECTIVE VIEW

41

It is a common remark that every design must necessarily be bad in which the peculiarities of more than one style are introduced. According to general opinion, the national architectures must not be blended with each other, or, in other words, there must be no attempt at improvement. This is an error which seems to pervade society in reference to architecture. Men who have received their notions from the usual method of expression employed by architectural writers, and self-constituted judges, entertain the firm conviction, that the introduction of any member or detail not used by the Grecians would render a structure, however closely it might otherwise be to an imitation of the style adopted by that people, a bastard composition. The importance of removing this erroneous opinion cannot be over-rated; for if a servile copying of the ancients be forced upon modern architects, what can be expected but a continued series of failures? By styles of architecture are meant characters; and these so blend with one another that it is extremely difficult to say where one terminates and another begins. Men of science informed us a few years since, that white solar light was composed of seven differently-coloured rays; but modern investigators have proved that there are only three primitive rays, and that, by the mixture of these, four other colours are produced. So there may be a definite number of characters in architecture, but by the admixture of these, an indefinite number of good designs may be produced. The human passions are but few in number, and yet, when blended, they produce an almost infinite variety of character. It is not, however, possible that a man should be both benevolent and cruel; and it is equally impossible that an edifice should produce upon an observer opposite feelings. All, then, that is to be attempted by the architect, or can be expected by the public, is, that there should be a unity of design, and that the character of the edifice, whatever it may be, should be maintained throughout.

The design represented in Plate XXXI. is an attempt to combine some of the characters of the Elizabethan and old English styles, and will, it is hoped, practically illustrate the remarks we have made.

It is intended that the building should consist of a stone plinth, with wood angular posts, sills, heads, and quarterings with brick nogging between, and the usual plastering inside and out.

In all edifices, and not the least in villas, the stair-case is a principal feature of the interior. It should, therefore, be always proportioned to the size of the house, and ought to be constructed in a style having some similarity to that adopted for the exterior. It may always be decorated with ornamental balusters, newels, and stringings, so as to have an exceedingly pretty or grand appearance, and impart a pleasing feature to the entire arrangements. In all the designs given in this book we have attempted to keep up the several styles which have been adopted through every portion of the edifice, and to introduce such ornaments as may be provided at a small cost, at the same time taking care that they should be in proper keeping with villa architecture. Too frequently a good design loses all its character from the redundance of ornament, or the want of propriety between one part and another. On the other hand, a meagre distribution of ornament, and a neglect of style in the preparation of parts absolutely necessary, is a fault scarcely less common. If we have avoided these opposite evils, the extreme faults, we shall not be denied that approbation for which we have laboured.

In Plate XXXIII. we have introduced a perspective view of a stair-case appropriate for the villa represented on Plate XXXI. From this sketch, the reader will at once perceive how important an object in interior decoration the stair-case may be made; and this may be done by appropriating a sufficient space, and introducing a little ornament suited to the style of building.

The same sketch will enable the reader to form an idea of the beautiful and noble appearance of the hall, corridors, and vestibules, from whatever point we may view the long range of passage; the elevation of which is heightened, and the length apparently increased, by the occasional arches. In the erection of such an edifice as that we have here designed, these things must be carefully considered; and the architect should not allow himself to be interfered

with in the manner of finishing his plans. We know too well that the proprietor will frequently attempt to thwart his intentions by insisting upon alterations which the professional man well knows will not be either creditable to himself or satisfactory to the employer. A man who consults his own character will first attempt to show the error, and, if unsuccessful, will rather decline the engagement than take the risk of subsequent discredit.

While speaking on this subject we may venture to give a little advice to both the architect and the employer. The architect is evidently engaged because the person who intends to build has not skill to design the edifice required, but has confidence in the skill, taste, and integrity of another. It is the first duty of the architect to consult the wishes of his employer, and to design so that he may obtain all the convenience required, at a cost not exceeding the sum intended to be spent. This being done, no liberty should be taken with the design in any particular, and especially in such parts as the architect may consider essential for the production of the effect he desires. It is the duty of the architect to accommodate himself, not only to the wishes, but also to the whims of the employer; but it not unfrequently happens that the control is taken out of his hands, and orders are given without his sanction, and contrary to his judgment. Under such circumstances it is wisdom to decline any further interference. The same remarks apply to the builder; and the employer may learn, that when a professional man is engaged, his authority should always be sustained—not usurped.

Plate XXXI.

Figure 1. Is the principal elevation.

Figure 2. Is the ground plan.

Beneath the ground floor it is intended there should be a kitchen, scullery, larder, servants' hall, housekeeper's room, wine, ale, and beer-cellars, with all the other necessary offices. The ground or principal floor consists of an entrance-porch, 9 feet by 5 feet; vestibules, 11 feet square; corridors, 17 feet by 11 feet; hall, 20 feet by 11 feet; dining-room, 30 feet by 20 feet; saloon, 23 feet by 20 feet; drawing-room, 30 feet by 20 feet; library, 25 feet by 22 feet; conservatory, 48 feet by 15 feet; principal stair-case, 20 feet by 15 feet; servants' stair-case, 20 feet by 8 feet. The height of this story is 12 feet.

In front of the principal elevation there is a terrace which extends 20 feet in length, and may be laid out in walks and shrubs. In front of each of the bay windows, which have casements opening on the terrace, a bold and handsome flight of steps is introduced. In the centre of the terrace, opposite to the saloon, with which it is connected by similar casements, a fountain is proposed.

The principal entrance to the villa is through a porch communicating with the vestibule, corridor, hall, &c., extending the whole length of the building, and terminating with a conservatory, producing a vista of beautiful appearance. In the centre and on the right is the principal staircase.

Plate XXXII.

Figure 1. Is the entrance elevation.

Figure 2. Is the first-pair plan.

Plate XXXIII.

Is a perspective sketch of the principal stair-case.

As this design is one of an extensive character, it has been thought necessary, for a full explanation, that it should be illustrated in six plates instead of three. The description will, therefore, be continued in the following pages.

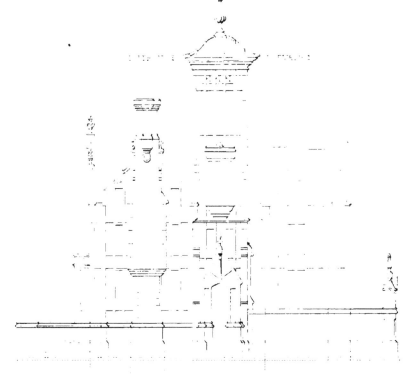

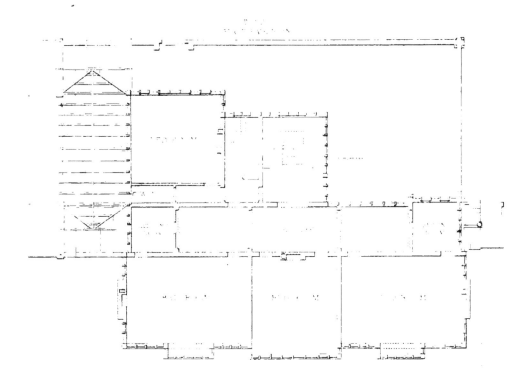

When a person has resolved to erect a building of any kind, his first consideration must be to select some suitable material. This will not be an inappropriate place to make a few remarks upon the mineral substances which are, or may be, employed in the construction of edifices suited for public or private use.

The substance of which a building is formed must, in nearly all cases, be chosen according to the mineral productions of the country in which it is to be erected, or the facility of conveying to the spot the building materials of another locality. A compact sandstone is, for the majority of purposes, by far the best material that can be employed. In the use of this substance, however, the greatest possible care is required. In siliceous sand-stones, the coarseness or fineness of the grains is, generally, of much less importance than the character of the uniting medium. Those varieties in which ferruginous clay is the uniting substance, are peculiarly liable to perish from exposure to the atmosphere: other specimens have their parts so loosely united together as to be altogether unfit for architectural purposes; to this class belongs the sand-stone rock on which the town and castle of Nottingham are built. The stones which are purely siliceous are less liable than any others to decomposition. Those varieties which scale off have that property from the admixture of other materials and the method of crystallization.

Calcareous stones include all the different kinds of lime-stone, from the most crystalline marble to common chalk. Some lime-stones consist of calcareous earth combined with magnesia, which commonly gives a yellowish tinge to the mass; these varieties dissolve slowly in acids, and are durable when used as building materials. The Bath oolite, or roe-stone, is extensively employed by architects; for it is carved with little labour, and has a light elegant appearance when finished. In spite of these advantages, however, we cannot but admit that it is porous, and not durable; so that the fine face is as easily destroyed by the weather as it is produced by the carver; and for this reason it should be rejected by those who have a regard for their future and posthumous fame.

An excellent stone is obtained from the hills near Dunstable, which, though soft when first brought from the quarry, hardens rapidly by exposure to the atmosphere. We may also state that it is durable, for it was used in the erection of Woburn Abbey.

From what has been here stated, we learn that there are some stones which, *in situ*, or when first obtained by blasting the rock, are so hard as to resist the pick, but peel off into small scales, or absolutely crumble when exposed to the air; while others, which are soft enough to be cut with a pen-knife when first obtained, become hard and durable when they have been acted on by the atmosphere for a short period.

Portland and York stones, so called from the localities where they are found, are extensively used in building; the latter for paving chiefly, and the former for sills, paving, and the better class of mason's work.

Granite is another stone commonly employed in building for those situations where great weights are to be carried. In the lower portions of warehouses intended as the receptacles of excessively ponderous goods, in bridges, and other works, it is introduced as the rock most capable of sustaining enormous pressure, and least liable to decomposition from the atmosphere. Granite is chiefly composed of quartz, feldspar, mica, and hornblende, three of which simple minerals enter into its composition. According to the proportions in which these unite, and the qualities of the preponderating mineral, will be the durability of the mass. All those specimens having a large amount of quartz, provided its crystallization be not an objection, are well suited for the purposes of the builder. If feldspar predominate in any mass, it should be rejected, for it is liable to decomposition from the atmosphere. Geologists inform us, that in the south of France, and in other localities where this variety abounds, the rocks are completely disintegrated, and the surface of the districts appear, to casual observers, as though they were covered with a loose gravel.

These general hints may be of some service to the builder in directing his selection of materials.

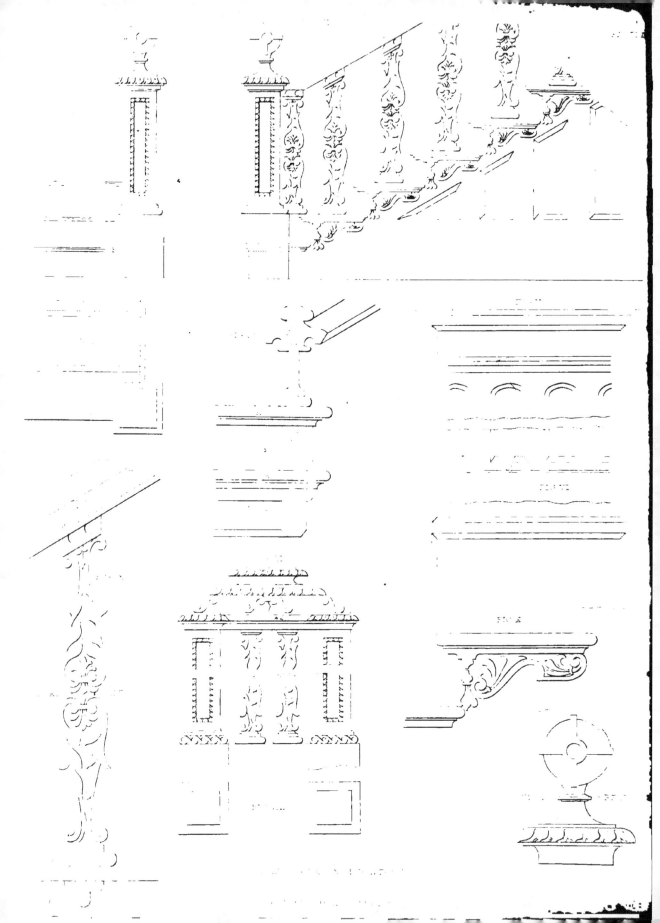

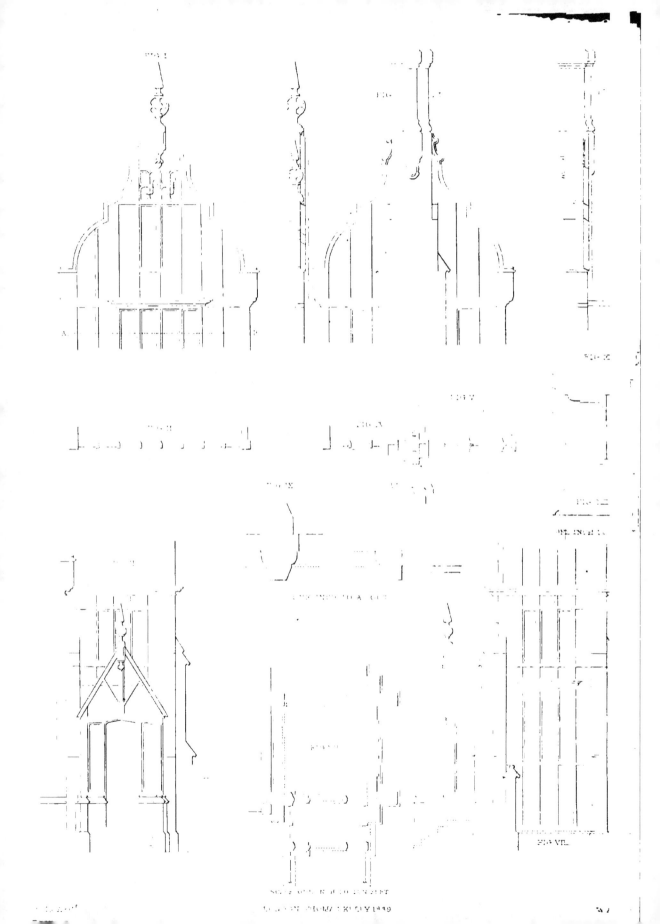

47

DETAILS.

Plate XXXIV.

Figure 1.—The elevation of the oak newel.

Figure 2.—The plan of the same.

Figure 3.—The side elevation of the oak newel, hand-rail, balusters, &c.

Figure 4.—Section of hand-rail, one-eighth the real size, showing the method of fixing the iron balustrade to the hand-rail, as well as to the tread of stairs.

A. Tread.   B. Riser.   C. Oak joist under soffit of stairs.   D. Plaster under the same.

Figure 5.—Plan of the method of dividing the panels of the soffit with the oak bearings.

Figure 6.—Elevation and section of the dado round the stair-case.

Figure 7.—The newels and finial of the stair-case on the landing.

Figure 8.—Plan of the same.

Figure 9.—One of the metal balusters, one-eighth the real size.

Figure 10.—One of the brackets of stairs to the same scale.

Figure 11.—Cap and ball to one of the newels, drawn to the same proportions.

Plate XXXV.

The details on this plate are for the external finishings, and are prepared to a scale of 1 inch to 10 feet, except those otherwise described.

Figure 1.—Gable end to the principal front.

Figure 2.—Plan of the same in the line A B.

Figure 3.—Gable end to entrance front, showing the elevation of the chimneys.

Figure 4.—Half plan of the same.

Figure 5.—The method of finishing the same.

48

Figure 6.—Elevation of entrance-porch and part of the tower.

Figure 7.—Plan of the same.

Figure 8.—Side elevation of part of the tower and entrance-porch.

The following details are drawn to a scale of one inch to the foot:

Figure 9.—Plan of mullion to principal windows.

Figure 10.—Jamb of the same, showing the grounds and architraves.

Figure 11.—Head of the windows.

Figure 12.—Sill of the same.

Figure 13.—Section of the gable end to entrance front.

Plate XXXVI.

Figure 1.—Elevation of the top of the tower. The scale employed is 1 inch to 10 feet.

Figure 2.—One of the piers to the terrace.

Figure 3.—Plan of the same.

Figure 4.—Elevation of the angular bell-turret.

Figure 5.—Plan of the same.

Figure 6.—Elevation of a portion of the tower, showing the bay window.

Figure 7.—The plan of the bay window.

Figure 8.—Chimney-piece for one of the principal rooms.

Figure 9.—Chimney-piece for one of the secondary rooms.

The following details are to a scale of one-eighth of the real size:

Figure 10.—Acroteria of bay window.

Figure 11.—Cornice for principal rooms.

Figure 12.—External cornice over windows.

Figure 13.—Cornice of ceiling for secondary rooms.

This building may be executed for the sum of about £4800.

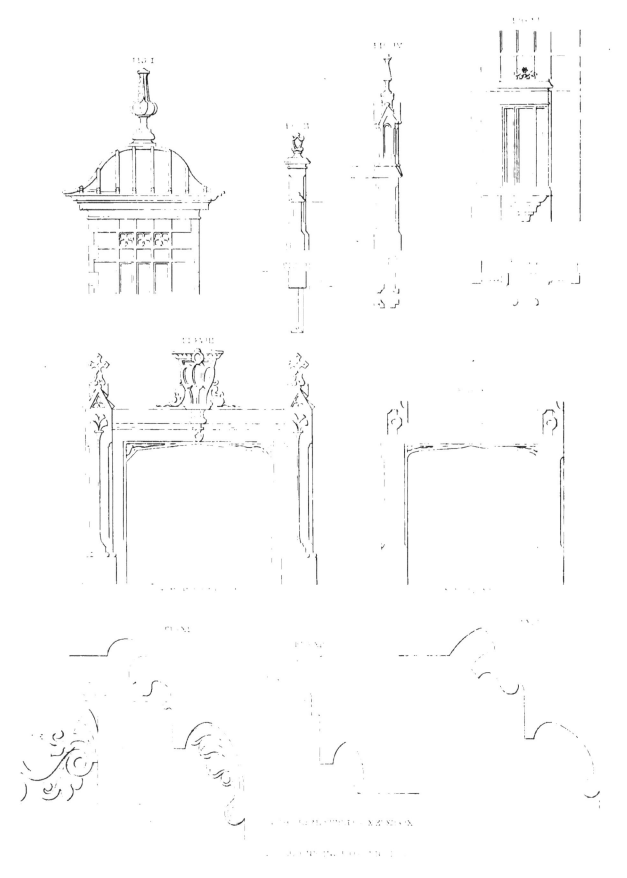

49

It is only within the last thirty years that any great attention has been paid in this country to the cultivation of the simple and classical styles of Grecian architecture; and in a few very remarkable instances, the designs of some of our most eminent architects have been executed in such a manner, as distinctly to demonstrate, that they were indebted to the original conceptions of the Greeks for that degree of beauty for which those designs are conspicuous. It must, however, be acknowledged, that Grecian architecture, from which the most splendid constructions of later ages have been derived, had its origin in the wooden hut or cabin, formed of posts set in the earth, and covered with transverse poles and rafters. Its beginnings were founded on the simplest rules, being little more than imitations in stone of the original posts and beams. By degrees, these were modified and decorated, so as to give rise to those distinctions now called the *Orders* of Architecture. By the Architectural Orders are understood certain modes of proportioning, and decorating the column and its entablature. They were in use in the best days of Greece and Rome for a period of six or seven centuries, were lost sight of in the dark ages, and were again revived by the Italians at the time of the restoration of letters, and are now inseparably incorporated with architectural science.

The most remarkable public edifices of the Grecians were their temples, which, being intended as places of resort for their priests, rather than for the convening of assemblies within them, as in our times, were for the most part obscurely lighted. Their form was generally of an oblong square, which has been almost universally adhered to in the erection of our modern churches, having a colonnade without, and a walled cell within—the cell was usually without windows, receiving its light only from a door at the end, and sometimes from an opening in the roof. The colonnade was subject to a great variety in the number and disposition of its columns, from which seven different species of temples have been described. For their Villas, the Grecians adopted a less expensive style, and for their smaller dwellings ornaments were entirely dispensed with; depending only upon the outline of the building, and

P

the plain, but fine contour, for the general effect. The pure Grecian architecture is gradually prevailing in this country, because the style is founded on plainer principles than any other, and because it is in reality better adapted than the Gothic to small buildings, nor does it require large and splendid edifices in order to display all its beauties. It is to Grecian architecture that we, are indebted for those elegant borders, which are what we call *grotesques ;* but with which the Grecian edifices were covered, representing mythological or historical subjects.

The Grecian edifices were not only in general very durable, but they moreover displayed the most beautiful proportions. The roofs were of timber, covered with tiles of burnt clay or marble. The larger edifices had flat timber coverings ; but the smaller ones, like the outward colonnades, were covered with stone : the Grecian columns, however, were far more graceful, and had a much less diameter than the Egyptian, for, in comparison with their African prototypes, they had no heavy burden to support. The want of timber coverings, and the necessity of employing large stone masses in the Egyptian architecture, will account for the horizontal covering of the inner rooms and colonnades, as well as of the doors and windows.

In the design represented in Plate XXXVII. we have endeavoured to adhere closely to the principles of Grecian architecture in its most improved and ornamental style ; and it will be admitted, that from its just and well-regulated proportions, and general boldness of design, an imposing effect is produced, arising from the distinct and various undulations of the outline against the horizon, as well as from the projections upon the different plans. Having given two geometrical elevations, three plans and a section, it has not been considered necessary to show it perspectively, which undoubtedly would have made the design appear to greater advantage to those acquainted with perspective ; but a geometrical elevation is by the majority far better comprehended.

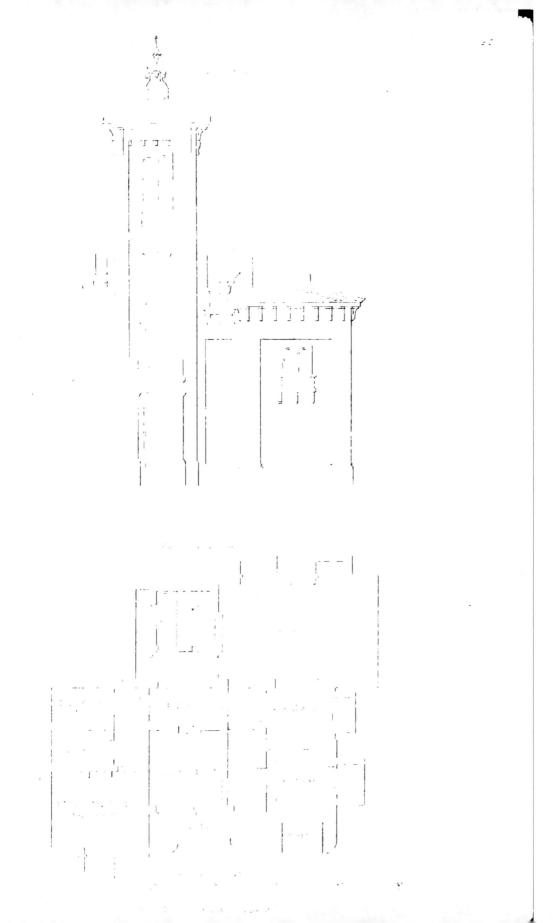

51

Plate XXXVII.

Contains the basement plan and geometrical elevation of the entrance front for a design of a small Grecian villa; and although columns and pilasters have been dispensed with, it will, viewed as a whole, have a pleasing appearance. The basement plan consists of a kitchen, 24 feet by 15 feet; scullery 10 feet by 9 feet; larder 10 feet square; butler's room 12 feet square; servants' bed-room 15 feet by 12 feet; ale-cellar 10 feet by 6 feet; and a wine-cellar of the same dimensions; stair-case, water-closet, &c. This story, from floor to ceiling, is 9 feet high. The butler's room and servants' room should be boarded, and the other apartments may be covered with asphalt, stone, or brick. Particular attention should at the same time be paid to the drainage, ventilation, &c. The external walls should be carried up from this floor to the under side of the ground or principal floor, two bricks, or eighteen inches thick; the internal walls may vary according to their different positions; the walls for the areas may be built either vertical or inclined, care at the same time being taken that the surface and other accumulated waters be properly conveyed into the various drains, &c.

Plate XXXVIII.

Exhibits the principal elevation and ground plan. It may be proper to observe that this elevation is in the position of the plan, but not so in the preceding plate; and this observation is applicable to most of the plans and geometrical elevations, in consequence of arranging the plans on the paper in the same position'; therefore when two geometrical fronts are shown, one of them cannot be ruled up from the position of the plan. The ground plan consists of a dining-room 25 feet by 15 feet; drawing-room of the same dimensions, communicating with a library by suspending doors, 18 feet by 15 feet; entrance porch 7 feet by 5 feet; hall in the space of the tower 10 feet square, which forms the entrance; the principal stair-case 10 feet by 10 feet, communicating with a passage leading to the principal rooms, lobby, servants' stair-case and water-closet; the hall and principal stair-case should be arched over and paved with stone; the other rooms may have joists 10 inches by 2½, herring-boned, trussed with an inch and a quarter bolt, taken through the centre to draw them to their proper bearings, sound-boarded and pugged, and covered with 1¼ inch floor-boards, dowelled with ploughed and tongued heading joints. All the external walls of this building should be battened with three quarter-inch battens, fixed at proper distances. Bond timber should also be laid at about every seven courses; and chain-bond should be introduced above the ground line, and under the joists of this building, which might also answer for the wall plate. This story is intended to be 11 feet high, with joists, &c., of the same scantling as described for the floor below, and finished in a similar manner. The architraves, doors, sashes, shutters, &c., should be finished as nearly in the character of the external appearance as possible— the style of which, as well as the cornices, are given in the succeeding pages.

Plate XXXIX.

The first-floor plan consists of three principal bed-rooms, with their suitable dressing-rooms, (two of which, from having a private communication, might occasionally be used as bed-rooms,) with principal stair-case, secondary ditto, and passage to water-closet, all properly and well ventilated and lighted. The attic plan is arranged for servants' bed-rooms, which, by a newly-invented construction in the roof, will give sufficient head room, &c. The roof may be framed with either wood or iron, and covered with lead, zinc, marine metal, or patent slates; care being taken to preserve the external appearance by rolls; a gutter may also be formed in the eaves in a similar manner to that exemplified in Plate XV.

Plate XXXIX. also shows the longitudinal section, taken on the line A B, marked on the ground and first floor plan.

This building may be erected for about the sum of £5000.

FIRST FLOOR PLAN

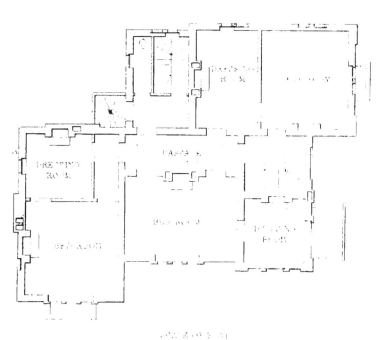

Among the many very useful species of timber grown in this country, we may especially mention the chestnut. It is the produce of a tree called by botanists the *fagus castanea*. It is said to have been brought into this country from Turkey; but it is, we believe, a native of all the warm mountainous countries of Europe. At some former periods it must have been very abundant in England; an opinion derived from the frequent mention of it in ancient topography, and its general use in old buildings.

Chestnut is a timber universally acknowledged to be very durable, so much so, that it is sometimes thought to be more suitable, as a building material, than oak itself. What foundation there may be for this opinion we will not pretend to determine; but we might point out many examples of its durability, such as the roof of King's College, Cambridge, and that of Notre Dame at Paris. In the old domestic architecture of this country it was extensively employed, and might be again with great advantage.

These remarks have been here made because chestnut may, with great increase of effect, be employed in the erection of the design represented in Plate XL. The principle of its construction is similar to that adopted in the design given in Plate I. of this work, and, in point of style, may be considered to belong to the old English architecture.

It is intended by the author that both the inside and outside should be lathed, the former in three coats of plaster and the latter finished in mastic or Roman cement. The space between the exterior and interior plasterer's work should be filled with sifted coal ashes, or any other substance that will absorb the moisture. The horizontal pieces should be placed about three feet apart, between the uprights, to resist the vertical pressure of the substance with which the interval between the plasterings is filled. These horizontal pieces should be framed into the vertical quarterings.

The hall and kitchen may be paved with brick or stone, and all the other rooms should be covered with $1\frac{1}{4}$-inch deals. The height of the ground-floor should be 9 feet 6 inches from the floor to the ceiling. In the preparation of the design the architect has had in view a suitable plan for a game-keeper's lodge, or a bachelor's residence.

As our space will allow, we will here introduce a few general remarks upon modern domestic architecture. The square or parallelogram, or a combination of either or both these figures, is better suited than any other form for a dwelling-house. For an edifice which is to have a regular and classical elevation the rectangular figure is to be preferred, but the length must not be more than one-third greater than the breadth, or the proper proportions will not be preserved. In villa architecture, however, the rectilinear form should, for the most part, be avoided, as a diversity in the lines of frontage produces a pleasing variety, and frequently gives an opportunity of adding greatly to the convenience of the structure.

The outline of the building being determined on, the interior must be so divided as to correspond with the character of the edifice, not only in the style of finishing, but in the distribution and size of the rooms. In a cottage the apartments must be small—in a mansion large. It would be much out of character to have an immense dining-hall in a secluded villa-retreat, and equally so to have nothing but small rooms in a large city residence.

The entrance to a residence should generally be in the centre, though in certain styles it is allowable to deviate from this rule; but there should never be more than one entrance, for not only is confusion produced by that means, but visitors are left in uncertainty as to the entrance most suitable for their degree or station in life.

If a house be intended to receive company, there should be, as it were, a double set of apartments; one for the use of the family, and one for the reception of visitors. The former should be of moderate dimensions, regulated by the number in the family, and fitted up with neatness as well as elegance; the latter should be spacious, and may be finished with more splendour than

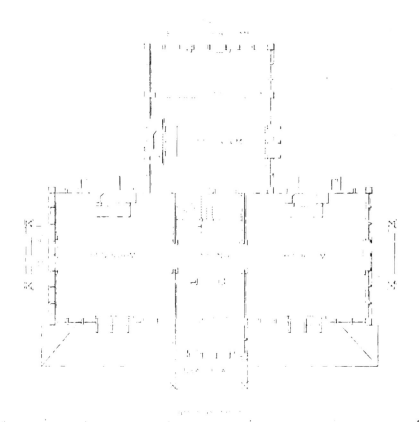

would be allowable for rooms which were to be constantly inhabited. The proportion of all rooms should also be carefully attended to. Rectangular figures are to be preferred, but the ratio between the length and breadth should not exceed 1½ to 1. According to some writers, the proportion between the height and breadth of a rectangular building should be about 1 to 1¼. In large public rooms, or such apartments in private residences as are intended to contain a large number of persons, should be more lofty, to afford a sufficient ventilation, as well as to give more effect to the decorations.

Plate XL.

Figure 1. Is a perspective view of a design in the old English style of architecture, showing the entrance front and the elevation of one end.

Figure 2. Is the ground plan.

Plate XLI.

Figure 1. Is a geometrical elevation of the principal or lawn front, showing the method of covering the thatched corridor, and of finishing the gable ends.

Figure 2. Is the chamber plan, containing three good bed-rooms, and a small room which may be used either as a library or dressing-room.

Three servants' bed-rooms may be formed in the roof. As the span of the roof is short, no principals will be required; couples and collar-pieces will be sufficient. The joists of this floor to be 9 inches by 2 inches, properly and securely fixed to the wall-plates. The couples to be 7 inches by 3 inches; collar-pieces 7 inches by 3 inches; purlins 5 inches by 2 inches; ridge-pieces 7 inches by 2 inches; common rafters 3 inches by 2 inches; batten for thatch 2 inches by 1 inch. The thatch is to be laid on at least 12 inches thick, and securely tied.

56

DETAILS.

Plate XLII.

Figure 1.—A portion of part of the barge-board, thatch, &c. sketched in perspective, exhibiting the method of securing the principal rafters of gable ends into the iron shoes which are bolted to the upright post and horizontal beam. A. Bottom of finial. B. Angular post. C. Iron shoe. D. Principal rafter of gable end. E. Horizontal beams. F. Thatch, which may be either of reeds or straw. G. Batten. H. Common rafter. I. Barge-board.

Figure 2. Is a geometrical elevation of the top of the same gable end, showing the finial. A. The top of finial. B. Thatch. C. Barge-board.

Figure 3.—A geometrical section of the barge-board, taken through the line D E.

Figure 4.—A perspective sketch of one of the brackets under the verandah.

Figure 5.—Sketch of one of the angular posts of the bay window.

Figure 6.—A geometrical section of the portico in lawn or principal front, showing the method of constructing the same.

Figure 7.—Another method of filling in ornamental angular pieces, introduced in the several gable ends, which may be either as here described, or as represented in Plate III.

Figure 8.—Cornice of ceiling for principal rooms.

Figure 9.—Cornice of ceiling for secondary rooms.

Figure 10.—Angular post for balcony.

Figure 11.—Plan of the same.

Figure 12.—Plan of window-frames. A. Centre mullion. B. Side mullion or jamb. C C. Casement frame. D. Window-post projecting 2 inches beyond the quarterings.

This design may be erected for about the sum of £457.

57

Much has been said by authors as to the advantage of some styles of architecture, in preference to others, in the erection of villas, but we are decidedly of opinion that each has charms of its own, and almost all possess a beauty of some kind or the other. Some styles being more suited to a peculiar locality, it is difficult to say which is, or which is not, the most beautiful. In the progress of this work we have endeavoured to select the beauties of each style; and by presenting to the reader a considerable number of designs, to give him an opportunity of selection. But we will here advance a few hints to assist the country gentleman in the choice of a style suitable to the site he has already chosen, or to direct him in the choice of one for a particular design. Each style of architecture has its character; and, by careful study, we are enabled to place it in the locality most in accordance with its characteristics. It would be absurd to build an Egyptian temple in a well-cultivated garden; and every reader must have perceived the impropriety of surrounding our magnificent Gothic cathedrals with the bare brick-walls of dark, inconvenient, and dirty dwellings, which seem to have been erected by men as destitute of reverence for the genius of their ancestors, and as avaricious of wealth, as they were incapable of appreciating the beautiful and sublime in art.

There are two characteristic distinctions in all architectural compositions; the prevalence of horizontal lines, as in Grecian architecture—or of the perpendicular, as in Gothic; but in each of these great classes there are numerous subdivisions. A villa in the Grecian or Italian style should be regular in its elevation, and be placed in an open situation, as upon a lawn, where the eye takes in the whole outline. The lawn should be diversified with parterres for flowers or very low shrubs, so as not to obscure the front; while only the inferior elevations, such as those of offices, should be hidden by trees, which also form an admirable back-ground for bringing out the entrance front. Opposite the door there should be a gravel sweep for carriages to turn; and, beyond, an open lawn, surrounded by trees, not in a regular curve, but broken by borders of shrubs: thus giving fresh interest to the view by increasing the variety in the tints of green, and allowing the rays of the sun to play in the distant vista. But if there be water in the vicinity, there should be a direct view from the house, with trees upon each side tolerably near; so that while the spectator is in comparative darkness, the eye may be fixed upon the bright reflected light from the water beyond. The drive up to the house should curve gracefully, but never entirely lose sight of the building.

If the locality be elevated or rocky, Gothic architecture should be chosen, particularly that which is castellated and of irregular outline; and picturesque shrubs may be easily so placed as to enhance the grandeur, beauty, or variety of the situation. If a tower form a part of the design, trees should be planted in such spots that on approaching the house only the highest parts may be seen; the edifice being thus raised in appearance much higher than it really is. The carriage-drive should then be irregular, sometimes emerging from among trees, and at other times almost buried in their shade; but at that point where the best view of the building is obtained, the drive should be open.

Picturesque knolls may be formed on the grounds, and every advantage be taken of each inequality of the surface. Some of the windows should look down the rocky steep, whilst from others there should be a view over the trees, commanding the scenery far beyond. But where the locality is rich and luxuriant, and partakes of neither the openness suited to Grecian architecture, nor the rocky character so admirably adapted for the castellated, a medium style may be found—that chaste and graceful Gothic which prevailed in the reign of Edward III., or the more luxuriant kind of later date. But there should still be a complete harmony of parts. The trees need not be so wild and sombre as the fir, but of a richer growth and foliage, like the chestnut, the elm, and the lime. The lawns should be of moderate dimensions, and gracefully diversified by shrubs and flowers, by walks, flower-beds, and grass-plots, so as to heighten the effect of the whole, and add new beauty to the edifice, if not to nature herself.

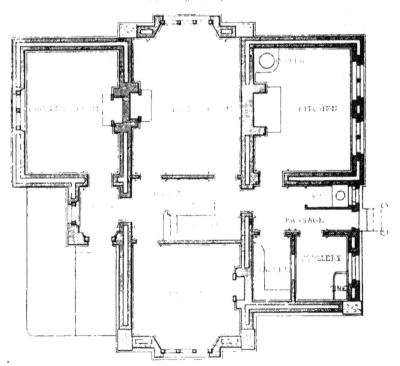

The design represented in Plate XLIII. is in the Italian style, and consists, on the ground floor, of a dining-room, library, and breakfast-room; and, on the one pair, of three bed-rooms.

Plate XLIII.

Figure 1.—The perspective view of an Italian cottage.

Figure 2.—Chamber plan.

In the construction of this building, it is proposed to erect the walls hollow by carrying up 4½-inch brick-work externally and internally, leaving a cavity between them of 5 inches. The bond of the brickwork is to be made by bricks, 14 inches by 9 inches, which may be placed every fifth or seventh stretcher horizontally, and in every third or fifth course vertically. In this way an excellent bond may be obtained, and if the sides of the openings be pargetted, in the same manner as fire-place flues, they may be made to convey rarefied air to all the apartments; and, with suitable ventilators, the rooms may be kept at an equal temperature, which cannot be done with a common English fire-place. To those who may require an equal temperature, either from choice or in consequence of ill-health—to those who suffer, during the inclement season of the year, from the coldness of one part of a room and the excessive heat of another, this method of building the walls will be of great value. The openings on the ground floor have, behind the fire-places, ventilators which admit cold air as may be required. This cold air passing behind an iron plate at the back of the kitchen, or any other fire, and by coming into a box prepared for that purpose, is heated, and consequently ascends the openings between the brick-work, and may be admitted by the ventilators into the various apartments as thought necessary.

The roof is to be of wrought metal, and should be constructed in a similar manner to that described in Plate XIV.

Plate XLIV.

Figure 1.—Elevation of principal front.

Figure 2.—Ground plan.

DETAILS.

Plate XLV.

Figure 1. Shows the method of constructing the brick-work hollow.

A. The opening, which must be pargetted. B. The bond brick.
C. The bond timber.

Figure 2.—Plan of the same.

A. The opening. B. Bricks. C. Bond brick.

Figure 3.—The method of fixing the stone-quoins, which, by being bedded in a shallow socket, will have an opportunity of settling with the brickwork, which is of the utmost importance in all buildings where stone and brick are connected together.

Figure 4.—Section of the quoin stones. It may be requisite to observe that it is not necessary to have all the bricks laid as stretchers, and as shown in the sketch; but the headers and stretchers may be laid, if considered more ornamental, in imitation of Flemish bond, and be equally as secure as the method we have particularly described.

Figure 5.—A section of one of the fire-places on the ground floor.

A. Ventilator for conducting cold air. B. Box and cavity for receiving the same. C. Fire-grate. The dotted line is intended to represent a wire that will communicate from the side of the chimney-piece to the external ventilator *c*. Immediately under this there is another, which by means of cranks will work upon both ventilators, and at all times, when required, give a brisk draught to the fire and prevent a smoky chimney.

Figure 6.—The external elevation of the ventilators.

This design may be executed for about £525.

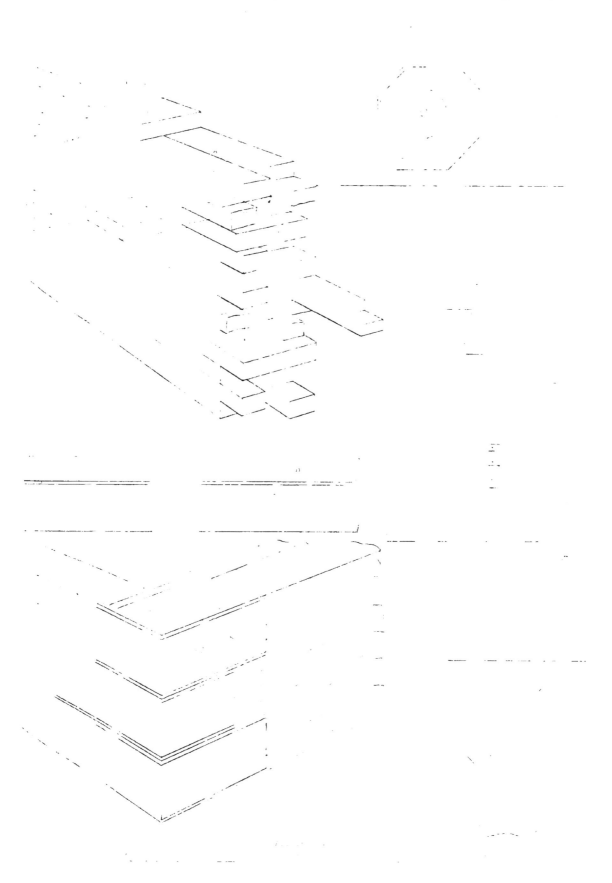

61

Those who are at all acquainted with national architecture, are quite aware that the architecture of all nations. originates, in a great measure, in the climate of the country, and the manners and wants of the inhabitants. Thus, in Egypt, where wood was scarce and stone abundant, the style of architecture was adapted to the wants and capabilities of the country. Large and massive stones were used in the construction of the temples, and the effect produced was cavernous, from the absence of windows and the closeness of the columns, which were of gigantic size, similar to the props which would be left in a subterranean excavation to carry the superposing masses. The Chinese architecture doubtless originated in the nomadic habits of the aboriginal inhabitants, the wandering Tartars, who lived in tents, which are the types of the Chinese style; for even on their roofs imitations of the cords of tents may frequently be seen. In Greece, where the air was serene, the sky cloudless, and rain infrequent, the roofs were low, and at a very acute angle. But in more northern countries, where snow and storms are common, the roofs were made high, that the rain and snow might be better thrown from them. In Switzerland the architecture equally illustrates the climate of the country and the manners of the people. From the inclemency of the weather the cattle must be sheltered, and yet the fierce gusts of wind which prevail in all mountainous regions would blow down any small sheds that might be erected. The cattle are therefore placed on the ground floor of the edifices that shelter their proprietors. This creates the necessity of approaching the upper or living apartments from the outside to avoid the animals, and at the same time produces the most picturesque characteristic of the style—the external staircase; whilst a gallery, supported by fanciful brackets, is usually continued round the house. The importance of sheltering this gallery gives rise to another peculiar characteristic of this style—the enormous projection of the roof, which often extends from eight to ten feet beyond the face of the wall. But to obviate the danger of so great a projection of the roof catching the violent gusts of wind which sweep around it, threatening to carry away the entire structure, they are compelled to adopt the clumsy alternative of placing large pieces of rock upon the outside, that their weight may counteract the influence of the wind. This, although contrary to the true principles of construction, does not look so clumsy as would be imagined by one who had never seen the structures themselves; for the spaces between the stones are in process of time filled with mould, and a soil is thus formed for the growth of a thousand wild flowers, producing a pleasing object for the eye to rest upon, while the reason is satisfied with the main object in the introduction of the stones, that of retaining the roof in its place, in spite of all the atmospheric causes which have a tendency to throw it from the walls. Few persons can conceive how picturesque these cottages appear in Switzerland. The wild beauties of all the physical features of the district, the rushing of the torrents, the deep shadows thrown by the hardy firs, and the snow-capped mountains, rising one above the other until at last the most distant is blended with the blue sky, form a scene so beautiful in detail, and so sublime as a whole, that the mind can have no conception of its power unless by experience.

Many persons have stated that the Swiss architecture is not suited to this climate; and there is some reason in the objection. We have, however, on more than one occasion, erected cottages in the Swiss style, in different parts of the country, and they have been thought to produce a picturesque and beautiful effect. The situation is of course to be considered, for the building must be consistent with the scenery. But we have dwelt, in other parts of this work, with some particularity upon the subject, and need not, therefore, repeat our remarks. It is only necessary to say, that those situations which have the nearest approximation to Swiss scenery are the best sites for Swiss cottages.

In Plate XLVI. is a design for a villa in the picturesque style prevailing in various parts of the Alps, but more particularly in Switzerland, and hence called the Swiss.

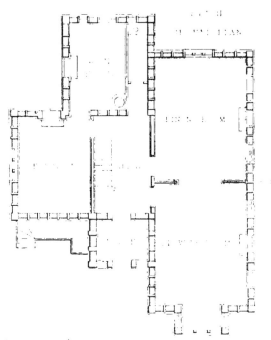

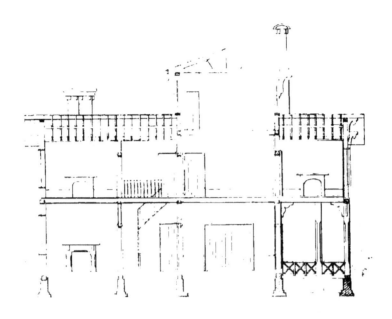

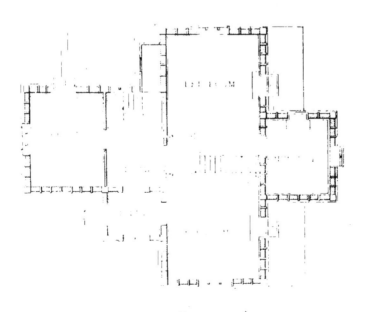

This design is intended to be erected of timber, and constructed in a similar manner to that shown and described in the first three plates of this work. The principal entrance is by a porch under a tower 8 feet square, connected with a hall. Here are the entrances, on the right-hand side, into the dining and drawing-rooms; and on the left, at the extremity of the hall, into the kitchen. Externally, there is a staircase, consistent with this style of building, leading into a lobby on the one-pair floor, from which there is access to the landing, and, consequently, to all the other apartments.

Plate XLVI.

Figure 1.—A perspective view of a cottage in the Swiss style.

Figure 2.—A ground plan of the same.

Plate XLVII.

Figure 1.—A longitudinal section, taken in the line A B, shown on the plan of the ground floor.

Figure 2.—The first floor plan.

The two principal bed-rooms on this story are 15 feet by 14 feet; the nursery is 13 feet by 11 feet; and the study, 15 feet by 12 feet.

DETAILS.

Plate XLVIII.

Figure 1.—A plan of one of the angular posts of the balcony.

Figure 2.—A perspective sketch of the same; showing the method of framing the cross-pieces of the railing. This is drawn to a scale of half an inch to a foot.

Figure 3.—A plan of the grounds and architraves for the door and windows.

Figure 4.—A perspective sketch of the chimney-top, to the scale of three-quarters of an inch to the foot.

Figure 5. Shows the method of fitting-up one of the principal rooms. The fire-place is of that kind formerly employed almost universally— that in which the fuel is burnt on metal dogs. This method of heating an apartment is now scarcely, if ever, adopted, although quite in character with the style of building, because of the insufficiency of the ventilation; but if the method we have proposed be adopted, there will be no danger of smoky rooms. For this method of heating and ventilating apartments, the plan we have already explained in a former page is peculiarly adapted, and neither the builder nor the proprietor need entertain the slightest fear of failure.

Figure 6.—A plan of the chimney-piece, showing the method of fixing and applying the framed dado and capping.

Figure 7.—Perspective view of lower part of the gable of roof, showing barge-board, bracket, wall-plate, &c.

This building may be erected for about the sum of £780.

It may be necessary to observe, in reference to our estimates of the several designs, that the cost of a building cannot be accurately determined without knowing the value of materials and labour in the place where it is to be erected. Much also will depend upon the style of finishing. Our estimates, however, are useful approximations, and will, it is hoped, be valuable guides to both the employer and builder.

From what we are able to collect from the Greek and Roman authors, and from an examination of those ruins which remain to our own day, concerning the methods of building adopted by the ancien's, it is quite certain they were accustomed to use both brick and stone, and these in different ways. For an explanation of the methods adopted by these people, we refer the reader to the account given by Vitruvius in the eighth chapter of his second book. In designing we can never far deviate from the proportions determined by the ancients without falling into error; but although their practice for a long time governed all modern works, and afterwards directed our inquiries, yet the advance of knowledge on all experimental and practical subjects has given us, in this respect, a station far above them. So highly did the Greeks and Romans cultivate the arts of design, and all the accomplishments of style, as well as the abstract reasoning powers, that we may, perhaps, in all these respects, be considered still as their scholars; and had they been acquainted with the method of interrogating nature by experiment, much that we have now the honour of discovering would have been found out by them, and our own intellectual condition would have been more advanced.

We shall not now dwell upon the different methods of building walls, as adopted by the ancients, but briefly state those which may be and are practised in the present day; especially in the erection of villas and cottages.

It is well known to every person who will read this work, that it is often necessary to introduce walls of lath and plaster, if we may so speak—or, as we are accustomed to say, partitions; and more particularly in houses where it is necessary to divide the area differently on the several floors. A similar plan may be adopted in the construction of an external wall. The laths are first covered with a coarse mortar, and afterwards with one which is finer, and when quite dry, painted or coloured.

Great care is required in the construction of what may be called a boarded wall. When this has been done, the external face should be painted, and the internal may be plastered. By the adoption of this method the structure may last for a long period, and the danger of accident by fire be altogether avoided.

Brick-nogging may also be introduced for the construction of walls, in some situations, with great advantage. When this method is adopted, both the external and internal face should be plastered, or the outside should be rough-cast with a composition of lime and fine gravel; and if this be done with care, the work will be enduring. This method of forming the external wall of a cottage will produce a good effect; for the contrast between the rough-cast and the timbers, which should always be painted of a dark colour, will be pleasing to the eye.

The design represented in Plate XLIX. is in a style of architecture closely resembling that of the Swiss cottage. It is proposed to be erected of timber, and to be completed in the same manner as the design represented in Plate I., except that the uprights are to be filled with flint or iron-stone instead of brick, and to have a stone plinth, and brick quoins and chimney-backs. In a district where flint-stones are plentiful and bricks scarce, this style of building may be adopted with economy, at the same time securing durability and a pleasing effect.

The method of finishing the chimney-tops in this and similar designs is of great importance, as they are conspicuous features of the style. The gallery over the porch, as well as the one in the front, may be omitted, if thought desirable, without materially altering the appearance of the building, which is, in every respect, complete without them, although they are exceedingly characteristic.

Plate XLIX.

Figure 1.—A perspective view of a design in the Swiss style of architecture.

Figure 2.—A ground plan of the building, consisting of a parlour

FIG I

PERSPECTIVE VIEW

GROUND PLAN

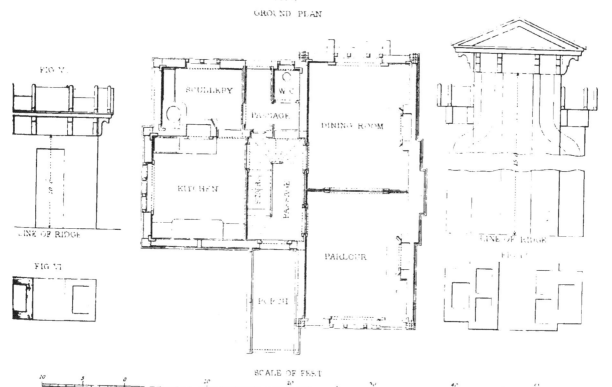

FIG V.

LINE OF RIDGE

FIG VI

SCULLERY

W C

PASSAGE

DINING ROOM

KITCHEN

PASSAGE

PARLOUR

PORCH

LINE OF RIDGE

SCALE OF FEET

10 5 0 10 20 30 40 50

LONDON THOMAS KELLY 1839

W. A. BEEVER

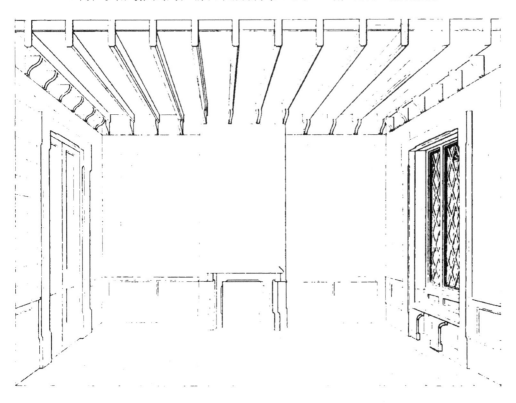

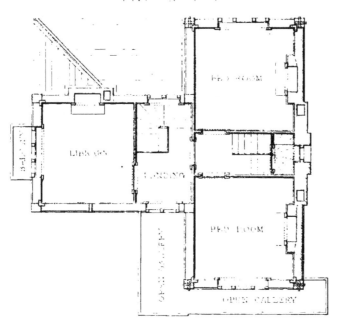

BED ROOM

LIBRARY

LANDING

BED ROOM

OPEN GALLERY

15 feet by 12 feet, communicating, by sliding doors, with a dining-room of the same dimensions; each of these apartments has a separate entrance to the passage and stair-case, which is 12 feet long by 8 feet wide. The kitchen is 13 feet by 12 feet, and communicates with a scullery 10 feet by 8 feet. The height of this story is 9 feet 6 inches.

Figure 3.—An elevation of one of the small chimneys.

Figure 4.—A plan of the same.

Figure 5.—An elevation of one of the large chimneys, which form a prominent feature in the building.

Figure 6.—A plan of the same.

Plate L.

Figure 1.—A perspective sketch, showing the method of finishing one of the principal rooms. The ceiling of this room must be finished in a similar manner to that we described when speaking of Plate XI., and the casements, doors, panelling, and other joiners' work, may be executed in the same style.

Figure 2.—Plan of first floor; which consists of a front bed-room 13 feet by 13 feet, and a back bed-room of the same dimensions; also a third room 13 feet by 12 feet, which may be employed either as a library or a sleeping apartment.

The attic story may be divided into two or three bed-rooms for servants.

DETAILS.

Plate LI.

Figure 1.—Shows a new method of fixing the angular wood post upon the stone plinth, so as to prevent the possibility of water getting into the stone mortice, and causing the decay of the wood tenon. A. Angular post. B. An iron ferrule to prevent the bottom of the post from cracking.

Figure 2.—A plan showing the stone plinth, the flint wall, and the internal brick quoin. C. Angular post. D. Flint wall. E. Stone plinth.

Figure 3.—A sketch of the angular stone. It will be observed that in this method the tenon is left in the stone to receive the post shown in Figure 1. F. Flint wall. G. Stone plinth. H. Tenon.

It may be here worthy of remark, that in this as well as all similar joints a small quantity of sheet lead should be introduced to cover the bed, so as to counteract any inaccuracy in the workmanship.

Figure 4. — One of the wood brackets, with planceer and cornice attached. I. Planceer. J. Bracket. K. Post.

Figure 5.—The wood palisade over porch. L. Angular post. M. Capping. N. Palisade. O. Lead flashing. P. Cornice. Q. Brest-summer. R. Post or upright.

Figure 6.—A geometrical section of the same. S. Hand-rail. T. Palisade. U. Boards of flat. V. Joists. W. Brestsummer. X. Post. Y. Cornice.

Figure 7.—Elevation of the entrance-door. *b.* Stone water-tabling. *ff.* Fan-light. *e.* Transom. *c.* Console. *d.* Door-post. *h h.* Top and bottom rail. *k.* Muntin.

Figure 8.—A section of the same, in which the letters apply to the same parts. In addition to these, we have *a.* Wall. *g.* Architrave moulding. *j.* Stone sill.

Figure 9.—A plan of the same door, showing the method of fixing.

Figure 10.—A new method of grooving the door, &c.

Figure 11.—The muntin of door, and method of fixing the linings.

It is estimated that this cottage may be built for about the sum of £520.

There is much doubt as to the origin of the arch. It is not found in the ruins of either Egyptian, Indian, or Persian architecture, nor was it used by the Greeks in the exterior of their buildings, although they were probably the inventors. The Romans employed the arch extensively in all their works after its introduction, which appears to have been about the reign of Augustus. The semi-circular arch was almost the only one employed by this people. It was in the middle ages, when Gothic was introduced as the national architecture of Europe, that various forms of the arch were employed, and the ingenuity of the workman was called into operation.

The skill of a bricklayer or mason is better exhibited in the construction of arches than in any other kind of workmanship, and the best artificers are, therefore, generally employed. Brick arches are either straight, circular, or elliptical, terms which, although improper in themselves, are commonly employed by all persons engaged in the art of building. A distinction is made, in common expression, between the words arched and vaulted, the former being used for those constructions which are narrower than the latter; but whether such distinctions be wise or not, we leave the reader to determine. By a straight arch is meant a form of brickwork, having the upper and lower surfaces parallel, and almost horizontal, the several joints being directed towards the centre. This method of laying bricks is frequently adopted over doors and windows. We have beautiful specimens of semi-circular arches in some ancient structures, such as the triumphal arches of Titus and Constantine, which are not the least interesting relics of Roman art. We are well aware that these ancient structures are not free from censure in the estimation of architectural critics, but they will allow that in regard to style and construction they are more deserving of praise than blame. No kind of arch requires more practical skill than that which is circular on the vertical surface and upon the, plan. But there is not so much difficulty in the construction of an arch of this design as is commonly believed. One of the principal things to be considered is the method of striking the front of the bricks, which if once properly understood, the practice will be comparatively easy. Another fact to be mentioned here is, that the soffit of the bricks in these arches must have the same gauge behind as before, to secure the strength and a proper key, so that there may be no inclination to any other centre than that which results from the gravity of the mass. The best practical directions we can give are, that after the arch has been divided, and the bond in front has been determined on, two moulds should be made to sweep off the wall. Two uprights of wood should then be introduced a little above the top of the arch. One should be fixed at the top, and the other be brought to the top of the courses as they gradually rise. With a rod closely attached to the two ribs, and having a point at one end, strike the top edge of every brick. In this manner the exact curve required for the wall may be determined.

An elliptical arch upon the same plan may be executed in a similar manner, so far as the front and soffit are concerned. Arches that splay in the jambs, and rise to the same height, may be executed by attention to the following directions. Divide the arches on both sides into an exact number of bricks, and having drawn the width of the wall, and laid down the arches on both sides, let fall perpendiculars from the ends of the bricks on each side, and draw parallel lines into each by the splay of the wall, which will give the exact size of the bricks in the soffit, and likewise the splay of the face of the bricks on both sides.

The arch possesses many advantages over the lintel when used in common openings, although it is composed of a number of pieces, whose chief bond of union is in their shape and position. It is, however, necessary that all the pieces should possess an uniform shape, that of a portion of a wedge; and also that the joints formed by the contact of their surfaces should point towards a common centre. In this case no one portion of the arch can be displaced or forced inward; nor can the arch be broken by any force which is not sufficient to crush the materials of which it is made. In arches formed of bricks, having the sides parallel, as they are frequently constructed, any one of the bricks might be forced inward were it not for the adhesion

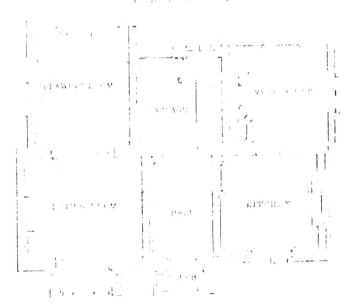

of the cement. Any two of the bricks, however, constitute a wedge by the disposition of the mortar, and cannot, collectively, be forced inward. An arch of the proper construction is rendered stronger rather than weaker, by the pressure of a considerable weight, provided the pressure be uniformly distributed. In turning an arch it is, of course, necessary that a system of framing, called a centre, of the shape of the intended internal surface, should be used to support the work until it is completed.

The importance of arches in every class of buildings cannot be over-rated, and it is scarcely possible to enumerate all the situations in which they are used in the erection of houses. The steps to entrances are generally carried on arches ; foundations have frequently inverted arches thrown under to give an extra stability ; and arches are thrown over window and door openings.

These remarks upon arches will, it is hoped, be generally useful to the reader, and are peculiarly applicable in this place, as will be perceived by the details we have given of a new method of constructing a fire-proof house.

Plate LII.

Figure 1. Is a perspective view of a design for a small villa, in a mixed style of architecture. The building is intended to be constructed on a principle which shall make it fire-proof ; the system of warming and ventilating, already described, being also adopted.

Figure 2. Is the ground plan, and consists of a dining-room, 15 feet by 14 feet, communicating with a drawing-room 16 feet by 14 feet ; an entrance hall, 11 feet by 8 feet ; a kitchen, 12 feet square, and a convenient wash-house.

72

Plate LIII.

Figure 1. Is the elevation of half the external front of the bay window to drawing-room.

Figure 2. Shows the method of construction, and the finishings of the inside of windows.

Figure 3. Is a transverse section of the window, showing the manner in which the plinth, sill, and balcony, are fixed or constructed.

Figure 4. Is a plan of the same.

Figure 5. Shows the method of fixing the cast metal casement.

Plate LIV.

Figure 1. Shows two methods of constructing fire-proof ceilings by means of metal girders and brick arches.

Figure 2. Is a method of constructing a slate gutter on the brackets.

Figure 3.—The string course.

Figure 4.—An iron or zinc gutter. Either of these metals may be employed with advantage as well as economy.

Figure 5. Is the plan of the first floor, consisting of three good bed-rooms and a dressing-room.

This building may be erected so as to be fire-proof, for a sum of about £835.

SECTION

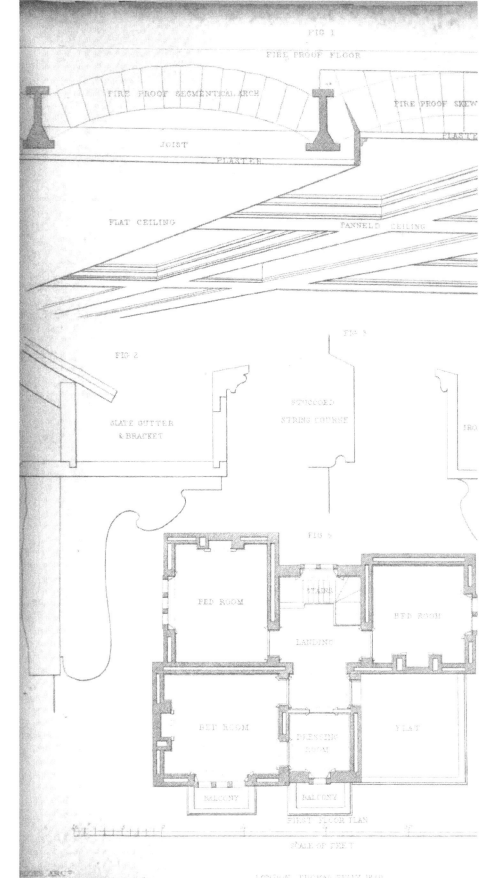

FIG 1

FIRE PROOF FLOOR

FIRE PROOF SEGMENTICAL ARCH

FIRE PROOF SKEW

JOIST

PLASTER

PLASTER

FLAT CEILING

PANNELD CEILING

FIG 3

FIG 2

SLATE GUTTER
& BRACKET

STUCCOED
STRING COURSE

IRON

FIG 5

BED ROOM

STAIRS

BED ROOM

LANDING

BED ROOM

DRESSING
ROOM

FLAT

BALCONY

BALCONY

FIRST FLOOR PLAN

SCALE OF FEET

LONDON THOMAS KELLY 1859

73

The old English architecture was, at one period, in great repute in this country, and was introduced with good effect in rural situations in the construction of villas. Many of the edifices then erected remain to the present day, and have recently been sought after, and described, in all their details, by architectural draughtsmen. The gable ends, so often found in old cities, although not strictly belonging to this style, may be studied with advantage by those who wish to design for this class of villas. The propriety of the style is evident, not only for its harmony with the freedom and variety of nature, but also because it recals to our recollection the times, manners, and prejudices of our forefathers. It has also the great recommendation that it may be adopted at a trifling expense, and the materials necessary for construction may be obtained in almost any situation. Here and there, in secluded spots, we have met with examples so unassuming, and yet so appropriate, that we still associate them with the natural scenery by which they are surrounded, and always fancy them necessary for the effect which was produced upon our mind. The rich decorations that have been introduced in some of the old specimens are not generally suited for the situations in which we should prefer to place an old English villa; nor is the style itself one suited to every country situation. Upon the open and extended lawn the classical architecture is most in character; in the park and forest, the baronial mansion of the Tudor style; but in the quiet sequestered nook, or by the edge of the forest, within sight of the mountain and waterfall, we would choose a site for our old English cottage. There are not many general readers who have the slightest idea, that for the appreciation of a design, it must be erected in a situation which has natural characters in some degree of accordance with the feelings and sentiments produced by the style itself. We might select many of the most beautiful specimens of rural architecture, which, if removed to other situations than those in which they are placed, would lose all their interest, and create in the mind of an observer sentiments very different from those they now call into activity. Nor would it be difficult to mention many buildings which, although in excellent proportion, and finished with care and propriety, are still destitute, as it appears

x

to us, of all spirit and character, and merely because they are erected in inappropriate situations.

The design represented in Plate LV. is in the old English style of architecture; a style remarkable for the irregularity of the plan, the frequent introduction of gable ends and dormer windows, and its adaptation to rural situations for cottages and villas. In all architectural designs it is of the greatest importance that the same character should pervade the whole, notwithstanding the difference there must necessarily be in the method of decorating the several parts. The difficulty of effecting this is so great, that by young artists it is frequently found more easy to adopt what they call a style of their own, or to blend the unfit members, proportions, and ornaments of their own invention with those of the style in which they intended at first to design, than to study the old specimens of architecture from which they might derive the necessary information. In the design now presented to the reader we have endeavoured to keep up the general tenor and character of the style, and the perspective view may be considered as a specimen of it.

Plate LV.

It is proposed that the cottage represented in this plate should be lathed and plastered between the uprights, externally and internally, the former in Roman cement, the latter in plaster. The opening between the two coats should be filled with saw-dust or sifted coal-ashes, to absorb any moisture that might pass from one surface to the other. Horizontal pieces should be fixed between the uprights, about three feet apart, to receive the vertical weight of the plaster. It is intended to pave the ground floor with slate, stone, or asphalte, the method of construction being suited to either of these materials. The brick piers and arches which are shown in Figure 17 of Plate LVII. should stand about 18 inches above the ground, and be about half a brick in thickness. These arches will carry the paving.

From the detail drawings it will be perceived that we intend the building should be covered with reeds or straw. The practice of thatching the roof of

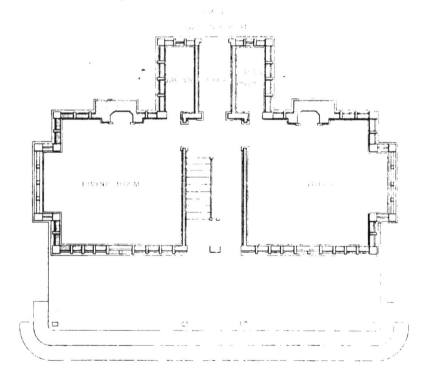

LIVING ROOM

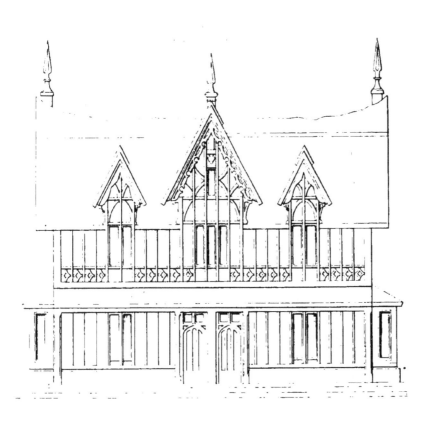

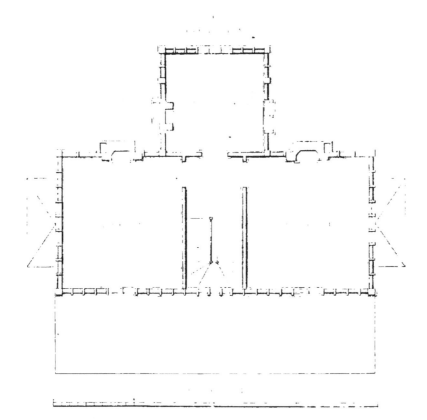

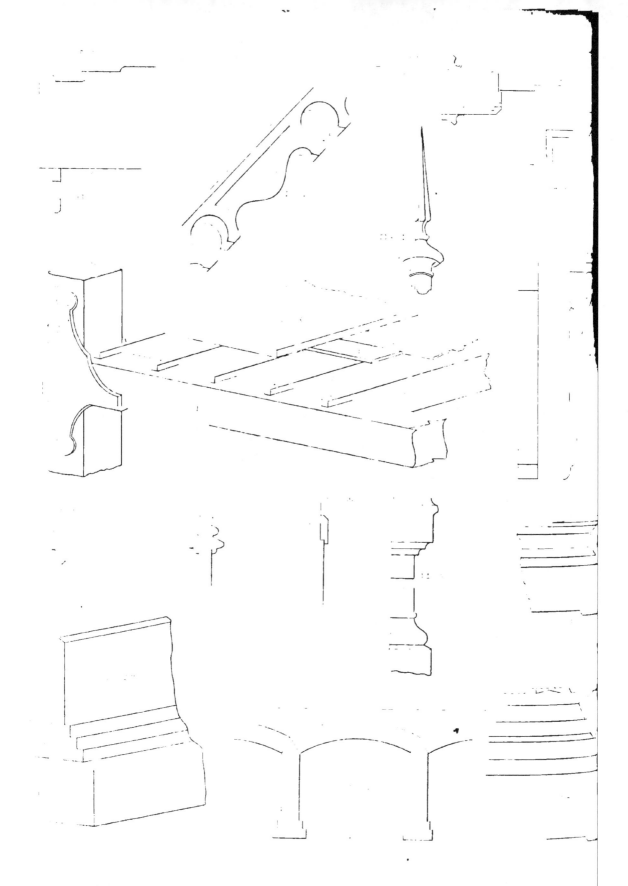

the cottage, and rustic villa, is now almost abandoned, but it is so suited to a particular style of rural architecture that we regret it should be so much neglected as to be almost forgotten.

Figure 2. Is a ground plan of the cottage, and is arranged as a residence for a game-keeper, gardener, or some other servant upon a gentleman's estate. This floor consists of a living-room or kitchen 16 × 15, and a parlour of the same dimensions. On either side of the entrance-lobby there is a larder or store-closet. A corridor or terrace extends along the entire front of the building on one side, and a geometrical elevation of it is given in Figure 1 of Plate LVI. The height of the ground story, from the floor to the ceiling, is intended to be 9 feet 6 inches.

Plate LVI.

Figure 1. Is a geometrical elevation of the principal or lawn front.

Figure 2. Is the chamber plan, which consists of three bed-rooms, the two front ones being 16 feet by 15 feet, and the other 12 by 12. There are also three rooms in the roof, but these are of minor importance.

This story is intended to be 8 feet in height, and is to be finished in a similar manner to the ground floor.

The span of the roof being small, no principal rafters will be required, couples and collars being quite sufficient.

The joists of the floors are to be 9 × 2½, securely fixed to the wall-plates; couples, 7 × 3; collars, 7 × 3; purlins, 5 × 2; ridge, 7 × 2; common rafters, 3 × 2; battens for thatch, 2 × 1. The thatch must be at least 12 inches thick, well laid, and securely tied.

DETAILS.

Plate LVII.

Figure 1.—A portion of part of the thatch and barge-board, to a scale of half-an-inch to the foot.

Figure 2.—A geometrical section of the same. A. Purlins. B. Barge board. C. Thatch.

Figure 3.—A section of plain cornice.

Figure 4.—A plan of door-frame and door.

Figure 5.—The bracket under over-hanging gable, drawn to a large scale.

Figure 6.—The pinnacle introduced on the gable ends, drawn to a large scale.

Figure 7.—The front view of the brackets under the window.

Figure 8.—The side view of the same.

Figure 9. Represents the angular post, with the method of framing the middle timbers into it, and also the method of fixing the joists, and of laying the floor-boards, slate, stone, asphalte, or whatever other material may be used. A. Angular post. B. Middle timber. C. Joists. D. Thin boards to be beaded on the underside, intended to serve the purpose of a ceiling. The boards will be seen between the joists, and the appearance will be much more in character with the general style of the building than a lath and plaster ceiling. E. An asphalte, stone, or slate floor.

Figure 10.—The moulding for the underside of the eaves.

Figure 11.—The handrail for the stairs.

Figure 12.—The skirting for the rooms.

Figure 13.—The mouldings for the chimney-top and base.

Figure 14.—A design for a cornice.

Figure 15.—Another design of a cornice for the principal rooms.

Figure 16. Represents the method of fixing the stone plinth upon the brick foundation. A. Stone plinth. B. Brick footings. C. Concrete foundation.

Figure 17. Is a section of the $4\frac{1}{2}$ brick-walls and arches for receiving the asphalte, stone, or slate floors.

This building may be erected for about the sum of £525.

The common English method of warming rooms by open fire-places has many advantages, and is decidedly more pleasing to our prejudices than any other system. It is true that all the heat received is by radiation, and that the temperature of one part of the apartment is much higher than another—on one side we may be scorched, on the other almost frozen. Still it must be remarked that universal equality is not the system adopted in nature, and should not, therefore, be aimed at in art. The sky is not always bright, nor is the atmosphere always temperate; change seems to be necessary for the support as well as the happiness of mankind. There are methods of heating apartments by hot air and steam, but no plan seems to us so suited to the habits and prejudices of the English as the common fire-place for dwelling-houses; and it is, perhaps, the best, if sufficient ventilation be provided.

Too little attention is paid, in domestic architecture, to the importance of a sufficient ventilation, and still less to the circumstance that it should be, as much as possible, under the control of the person who may occupy the dwelling. The want of sufficient ventilation is productive of many evils, which may, we believe, be entirely prevented by the adoption of the simple and economical principle we have proposed, which can be done during the construction of the building at a very small increase in the expense. In the majority of cases, a building is completed before any consideration is given to the process of warming and ventilating. The consequence of this is, that a large portion of the work must be afterwards taken down to fix pipes and other iron-work ordered by the engineer, by which the building itself is much injured, and a large sum of money generally expended. These evils might be prevented, and money saved, if the architect would take pains to provide a suitable method of warming and ventilating before the building is commenced, and prepare the necessary drawings with the same care as he exhibits in the plans, elevations, and sections. For many years practical men have been anxiously studying the best method of accomplishing these purposes, but none of the plans adopted by engineers are of general application; the system which is suitable for one building being altogether unfit for another. Hence it is that in almost every instance the plan adopted by one architect is considered either insufficient or injudicious by others.

Plate LVIII.

Figure 1. Is a design for a cottage in the same style of architecture as that represented in Plate I., and constructed, as far as regards the principal timbers, in the same manner. Instead, however, of placing the quarterings 12 or 15 inches apart, and filling the openings with 4½ inches brick nogging, it is proposed to build 9-inch brickwork between the several vertical timbers. In those places where windows are introduced, the wall must be 14 inches thick, so as to allow an opening of 4½ inches, to admit of the action of a newly-invented metal suspended casement and shutter, the construction of which will be presently fully described. The casement is a necessary characteristic of the cottage style here adopted; and yet many persons, conscious of the inconvenience it occasions, have dispensed with it altogether, and introduced sashes, which have completely destroyed the effect and ordonnance of the design. The author, however, is fully convinced, from practical observation and careful consideration, that a great improvement may be made in the construction and action of casements, so that they may be equally applicable to the mansion of a gentleman and the cottage of a husbandman. The result of our inquiries and thoughts will be understood by the drawings and descriptions which form a part of this design. The perspective view shows the entrance front and one end of the building. If a good sound brick can be procured, the openings between the timbers, being built in 9-inch brick-work, need not be covered with cement. The foundations should be laid 18 inches below the surface of the ground, and on concrete if the foundation should be so loose as to require it. Three courses of brick-work should be laid to receive the stone plinth upon which the sill is bedded.

Figure 2. Is the ground-plan. At the entrance of the house there are two steps, having a rise of 6 inches, leading to the porch. From the hall

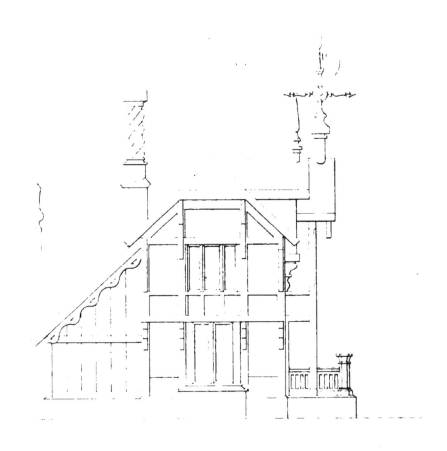

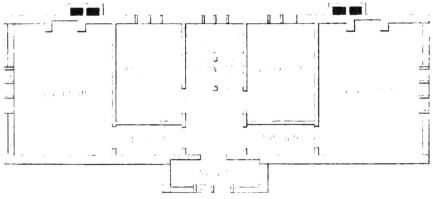

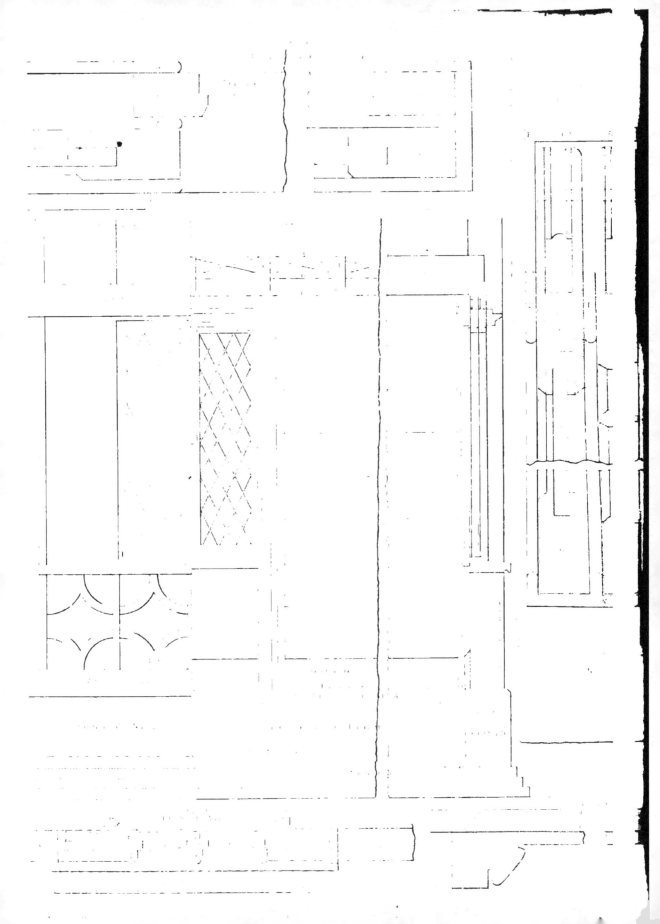

there is an entrance severally on the right and left-hand side into the drawing and dining-rooms. The same hall is connected with a passage leading into the kitchen and all the domestic offices. The space between the ground and underside of the floor is intended to be filled up with dry lime rubbish.

Plate LIX.

Figure 1. Is the end elevation drawn to scale, and all its details are sufficiently distinct to enable the builder to erect it with confidence.

Figure 2. Is the chamber plan, consisting of two large bed-rooms, 16 feet by 13 feet; two smaller, 12 feet by 11 feet. The joists for this floor should be about 9 inches by $2\frac{1}{2}$ inches. Three small bed-rooms for servants may be introduced in the roof.

DETAILS.

Plate LX.

Figure 1. Is a plan showing the method of fixing the metal frame, casements, shutters, &c., which will be explained by the following figures of reference :—

A. Brickwork. B. Sliding shutters. C. Architrave. D. Sliding casement. E. Mullions of window. G. Sill of window.

Figure 2. Is the half of the inside elevation of the same, showing the method of laying the floor of the ground story, as well as that of the one pair, which explains the method of fixing the herring-bone strutting, and of bolting the joists together. The construction of the first pair, or chamber floor, will be understood by the following reference to the letters by which the several parts are distinguished.

BB. Joists. DD. Iron bolts. CC. Herring-bone strutting. A. Floor boards. E. Ceiling joists and plastering.

Figure 3. Is the external elevation of the window.

Figure 4. Is a section of the window, to the same scale.

Figure 5. Is a full-size drawing of the cast-metal frame, casement, and shutters, showing the method of suspension by rollers on rods.

A. Wood Brestsummer. B. Cast-metal frame. C. Rollers. D. Suspension rods. EE. Parting rods. F. Top-rail of shutters. G. Top stile of casement. H. Casement Bar. I. Glass. J. Panel of shutter. K. Bottom rail of shutter. L. Bottom rail of casement. M. Bottom of cast-metal frame. N. Wood-sill. O. Space for carrying off condensed water.

Figure 6. Represents the back jamb of the metal frame, with the shutter and casement thrown back.

B. Window frame. G. Rail of casement. A. Stile of shutter. C. Panel.

Figure 7. Represents the middle meeting portion of the casement.

AAA. Parting beads. B. Stile of casement. C. Stile of shutters. D. Panel.

Figure 8. Shows the architrave for the doors and windows, half full size.

We estimate that this building may be completed for the sum of about £475, under ordinary circumstances.

The Greeks, as is perhaps well known to all our readers, invented three orders of architecture, the Doric, the Ionic, and the Corinthian; one being the representative of strength, another of simple beauty, and the third of ornamental, yet not too florid elegance. If we may believe Vitruvius, a Roman writer on architecture, the Doric, so called because the style was first used by Dorus, who built a temple to Juno in the ancient city of Argos, was formed upon the proportions of a robust man. In the Ionic, said to have been invented by the Ionians, the proportions of the female body were adopted. The volutes are said to represent the curls of her hair, and the flutings of the shaft the folds of her garment. The Corinthian column is intended to represent the delicate and elegant proportions of a young girl. We may with propriety entertain great doubt of the truth of the Roman account of the invention of the orders. But whether the tale that Vitruvius tells in regard to the invention of the Corinthian capital be a fable or be founded on truth, it is so probable and so pretty that we cannot omit it in this place. A young lady of Corinth died, and her nurse bemoaning her loss, strove to pay a token to her memory and record her own grief. Collecting together all the little trinkets which pleased the lady during her life, she placed them in a basket, covered with a tile, by the side of her tomb. The basket happened to be placed upon the root of an acanthus, which consequently grew around its sides, but being resisted by the tile, was forced downward, and the leaves curled at the ends, forming volutes. At this time, the basket, with its beautiful envelope, caught the attention of Callimachus, a celebrated Grecian sculptor, who was so delighted with it, that from this model he carved the capital of that order of architecture called the Corinthian. This capital is one of the richest and most beautiful ornaments of Grecian architecture; but, whenever the order is employed, great care should be taken to sustain the style, and to give an equally decorative character to the entire elevation.

The Romans, who adopted the three Grecian orders, desired to be themselves inventors, and, consequently, not only decorated the styles they had received from their masters in the art, but also proposed two varieties, which they called new orders. The Tuscan, however, is said to have been invented by the inhabitants of Tuscany, previous to any communication with the Greeks. But it must be evident to every one that it was derived from, and is a wretched imitation of, the Grecian Doric. The Tuscan order admits of no ornament, and is, in all its proportions, more massive than its prototype.

The second Latin order is a combination of the Ionic and Corinthian, but partakes most of the peculiarities of the latter. It is called the Composite.

The Ionic, which we have employed in the design, Plate LXI. is the most chaste, simple, and yet beautiful of all the orders, and has been more frequently adopted in modern structures than any other. This may, in part, be attributed to the simplicity of its decorations, and the comparatively small cost at which it may be executed. Nothing however can exceed the delicate proportions of the column or the elegance of the volute.

Plate LXI.

Figure 1. Is a perspective view of a design for a double house, suited for the residence of two families wishing to live as nearly as possible together and yet with separate establishments.

Figure 2.—A plan of the basement of one of the houses. This floor is intended to consist of a kitchen, 18 feet by 17 feet; scullery, 15 feet by 10 feet; servants' or housekeeper's room, 18 feet by 17 feet; wine and ale cellars, larder, and other offices, with front and back stairs. The height of this floor should not be less than 9 feet 6 inches; and all the rooms should be paved with stone except the servants' room.

Figure 3.—A plan of the ground floor, which consists of an entrance-hall, 10 feet by 14 feet; principal staircase, 20 feet by 10 feet; lobby, back staircase, and water-closet; dining-room, 18 feet by 17 feet; drawing-room of the same dimensions; and a saloon or library 17 feet square.

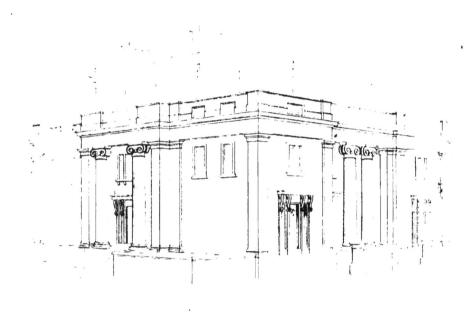

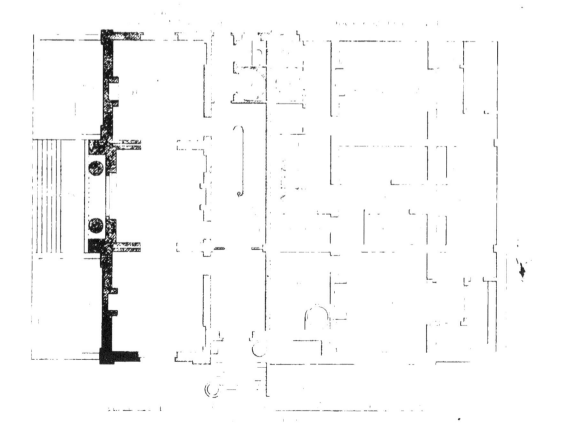

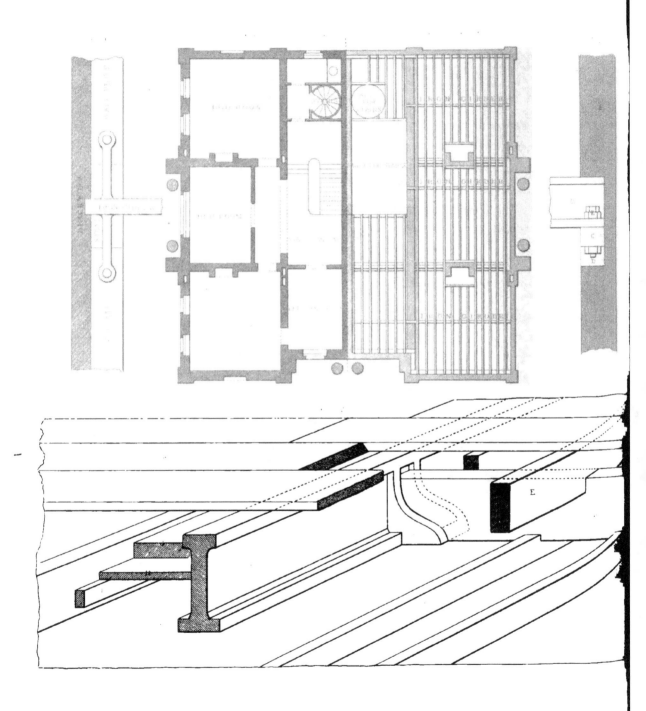

DETAILS.

Plate LXII.

Figure 1. Is a plan of the chamber floor, and consists of three bed-rooms and a dressing-room, all of which are approached by a bold landing from the principal stairs. In this plan a circular metal stair-case is introduced for servants, a convenience which cannot be over-rated in a family where several domestics are retained, and which may, in nearly all instances, be provided.

Figure 2. Is a plan of the naked flooring for the chamber story, showing the iron girders, joists, trimmers, and well-holes for stairs.

Figure 3. Is a plan showing the method of securing the metal girder to the bed of stone, and of connecting it by moveable flanges with the wall-plate, so as to allow for the expansion and contraction of the metal.

Figure 4. Is a section of the same.

A. The wall. B. Iron girder. C. Wall-plate. D. Stone. E. Metal bolt.

Figure 5. Is a perspective sketch of the manner in which we propose to support the binders upon the cast-iron girders, as well as the method of bridging and notching up the ceiling-joists to the same.

A. The floor-boards. B. Iron girders. C. Shoe for binders. D. Binders. E. Bridging-joists. F F. Ceiling-joists. G. Pugging. H. Sound boarding. I. Fillet.

Plate LXIII.

Figure 1. Is a plan of the attics, consisting, like the first floor, of three principal bed-rooms, and a smaller apartment, which may be used as a bed-room or store-closet.

Figure 2.—Plan of the roof, showing the zinc flats and sky-lights.

Figure 3.—Cornice of parapet.

Figure 4.—Cap of antæ.

Figure 5.—Principal cornice.

Figure 6.—Cast-metal roll to receive the zinc covering. This roll is much to be preferred to wood, because it is hollow; and, if laid with a small inclination, it will serve the purpose of carrying off any water that may, by any stoppage, pass into it.

Figure 7. Shows the method in which the zinc is to be fastened round the roll, and of covering it with a sliding cap, so as to allow for contraction and expansion, at the same time making the work watertight.

Figure 8.—A geometrical elevation of the same.

The advantages of this method of laying zinc, instead of upon the wood rolls, will be apparent to every practical man. It must be well known that the practice of soldering zinc is decidedly injurious, in consequence of the great contraction and expansion of the metal; and it is equally well known that the wood rolls are, generally, in a short time, destroyed by the rain, which makes its way beneath the zinc covering.

Figure 9.—A cornice for the bed-rooms.

The two houses represented in this design may be completed for about £7350.

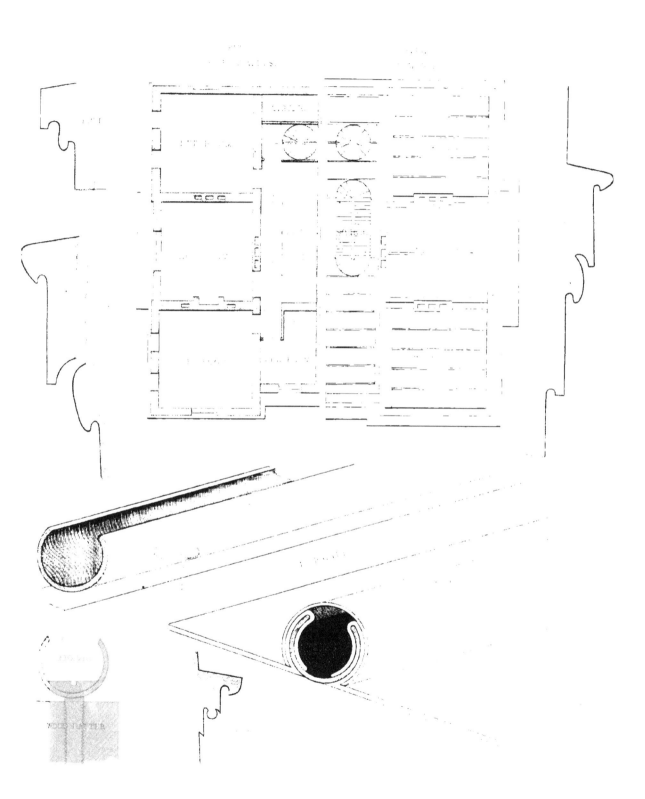

85

The several periods or styles of Gothic architecture are distinguishable in general characters, but in no particular more than in the form of the arch. In the thirteenth century it was lancet-shaped. In the fourteenth century the form of the arch was changed, for it was then constructed of an equilateral triangle; whereas, in the former period, the radius of each curved side was greater than that of the span. The vertex of the arch was thus lowered, but it was afterwards still more reduced; so that the radius was in fact little more than half the span. A still further change was introduced by the construction of the arch from four centres.

In the earliest specimens of Gothic architecture we find a great mixture of style, the Norman being so blended with the pointed that the peculiar features of each are in some degree lost. Hence it is that, in all our oldest cathedrals, the round Norman arch, and heavy zig-zag ornament and dark mouldings, are grotesquely intermixed with the light lancet arch and clustered columns of the early English. Instances of this may be observed in the Temple Church of London, the choir of Canterbury Cathedral, and Rumsey Church in Hampshire. Among the most splendid examples of the first Gothic period, that in which the lancet-headed arch was adopted, we may especially mention the south transept of Beverley Minster.

As to the precise time of the introduction of the pointed arch into the architecture of this country, no writer can speak with certainty; but we may introduce a remark, by Mr. Britton, peculiarly appropriate to the subject:—
" Were it possible to authenticate the very probable conjecture, that the Abbey Church at Malmesbury was rebuilt by that celebrated priest, warrior, and statesman, Roger Poore, Bishop of Sarum, we might then, with confidence, decidedly affix the introduction of the pointed arch to the reign of Henry I.; but, unfortunately, we are not in possession of any documentary evidence to verify this event. The ruins, however, of that church present so many of the known characteristics of the age of that prelate, and the circumstances of his life are so accordant with the supposition, that were it not from a firm resolve

to shun every approach to a controvertible hypothesis, there would be little hesitation in ascribing the building to his munificence. The great arches of the nave spring from very massive Norman columns, but are all pointed; while those of the triforium or arcade immediately over them consist, in each division, of four semi-circular arches, ranging beneath a sweeping elliptical one, ornamented with the zig-zag or chevron moulding. The label, or water-tables, over the archivolt of the large pointed arches, is ornamented with the billet-moulding, and terminated by heads of griffins or snakes." The earliest period of Gothic architecture commenced in the reign of Stephen, and continued through that of Henry III. and the intermediate periods—a term of about 140 years.

The second period of Gothic architecture may be said to commence with the reign of Edward I., and conclude in that of Richard II.; comprising a period of 105 years. Exeter Cathedral is a celebrated specimen of the architecture of this period; and also St. Stephen's Chapel at Westminster, which was erected between the years 1330 and 1348.

In the reign of Richard II. Gothic architecture received a considerable alteration in all its leading features and in its decorations. This third period extended to the early part of the reign of Henry VIII., and includes a duration of 140 years. The most beautiful specimens of this style are King's College Chapel at Cambridge, St. George's Chapel at Windsor, and Henry VII.'s Chapel at Westminster. Various names have been applied to the third division of the Gothic, such as the Tudor style, the florid Gothic, and the perpendicular; but none of these can be said to give the reader an idea of the peculiarities of the style they denominate.

The domestic architecture of the nobility in England was, for a long period, of a military character; but in the reign of Henry VIII. that style was superseded by a form of building of an entirely distinct character, and remarkable for the introduction of extensive courts and oriel windows. Hampton Court, which was partly erected by Cardinal Wolsey, and was commenced in the year 1514, had, when first erected, five spacious courts, although it now

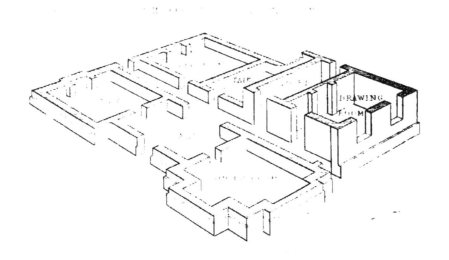

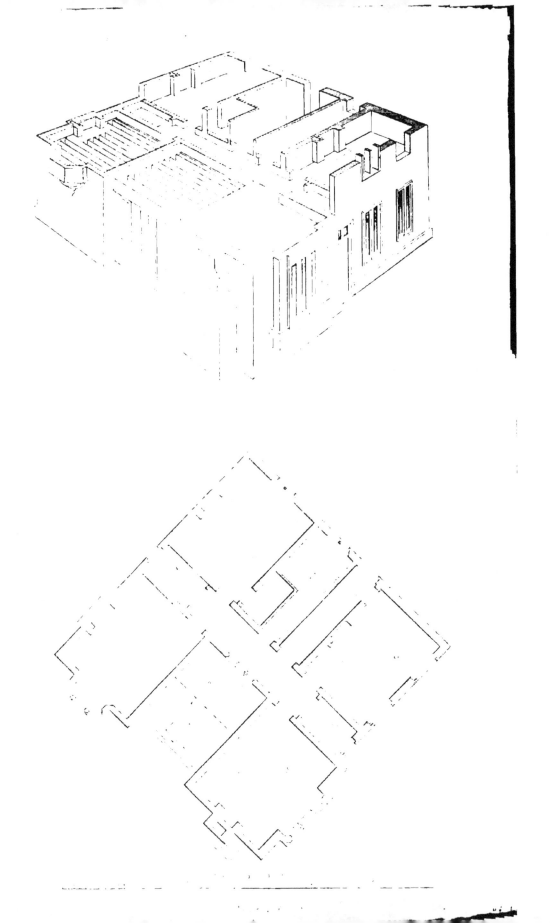

consists of only three complete quadrangles. The colleges of Oxford also are buildings surrounding quadrangular areas.

When the oriel window was first introduced cannot be determined, but it was certainly employed as early as the reign of Edward I. In the Tudor architecture, however, it became an important feature, and is still introduced in modern specimens of the style with great advantage.

In the design represented in Plate LXIV. we have chosen a period of Gothic architecture which is neither elaborate in its workmanship nor meagre in its details—and we anticipate that, when erected, it would present a graceful as well as a solid and imposing appearance.

Plate LXIV.

Figure 1. Is a perspective view of a cottage in the Gothic style of architecture.

Figure 2. Is a perspective plan of the ground floor, showing the walls, some of which are supposed to be carried to a greater height than others. This drawing will give an accurate conception of the appearance of the construction, when viewed from a given angle. The entrance-hall is 14 feet by 12 feet, and is connected with a passage which extends through the entire building. The dining-room is 17 feet by 14 feet; the drawing-room is of the same dimensions. A study, kitchen, closet, and stair-case are also provided.

Plate LXV.

Figure 1. Is a perspective view of the chamber plan, showing the lower portion of the building, as it would appear from an elevated situation. One portion of the floor is supposed to be laid; the other part shows the method of laying the joists.

Figure 2. Is a geometrical plan of the same floor. From either of the plans it will be perceived that there are four good bed-rooms, a dressing-room, and convenient closets.

The height of the ground floor should not be less than 10 feet, and that of the first floor 9 feet.

88

DETAILS.

Plate LXVI.

Figure 1. Shows a method of trussing a piece of timber from its own wood, which is a cheaper and more efficient method, for short bearings, than that in common use.

A. Represents a piece of timber 20 feet long. To truss it, a wedge, as shown at B, should be cut out of the plank so as to allow room for a saw-scarf to be taken longitudinally down the line C C. Small wedges are then cut out at the abutments D D, according to the camber which is to be given to the plank. An oak or iron wedge, and screw-bolt, as shown in Figure 6, are then introduced, as well as the two pieces forming the truss, which are forced up to the curve shown in Figure 2.

Figure 3. Shows a method of framing a double floor.

A. Girder. B. Bridging or floor-joists. C. Ceiling-joists. D. Fillet.

Figure 4. Shows the application of the same plan to roofs.

A. Tie-beam. B. Ceiling-joists. C. Fillet.

Figure 7. Represents a new method of securing the tie-beam to the wall-plate. By adopting this plan a sufficient play will be allowed for the vibrations of the floor or roof, and at the same time it forms as secure a tie as the old system of cogging.

Figure 8. Shows the method of fixing the truss to the oak or iron wedge, Figure 6.

Figure 9. Coping of water-tabling.

Figure 10. Section of the same.

Figure 11. Plan of window jamb.

Figure 12. Cornice of principal rooms.

Figure 13. Cornice of secondary rooms.

It is estimated that this building may be erected, according to the plans and elevations, for about the sum of £1275.

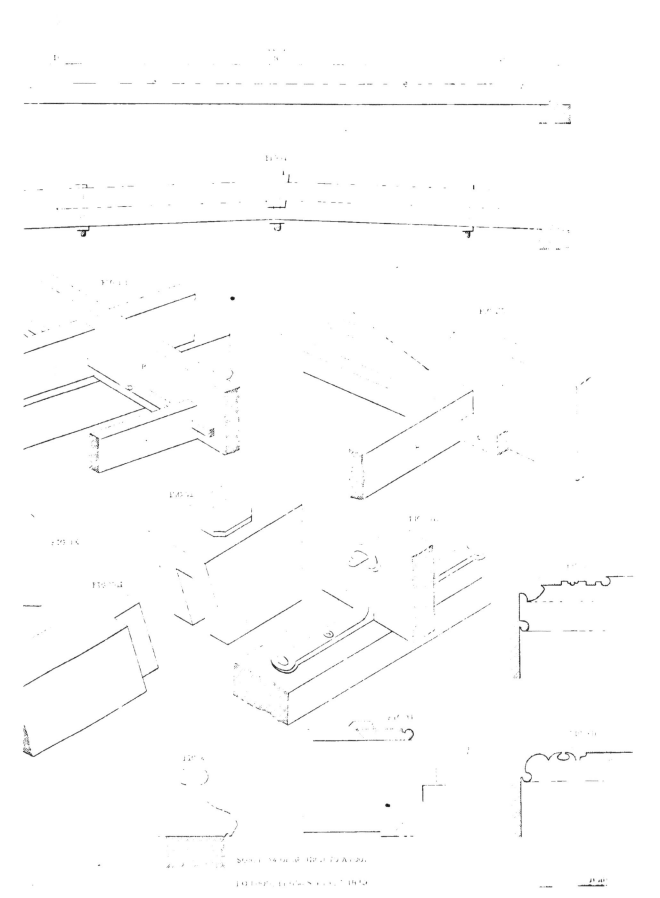

89

Writers on architecture have displayed great ingenuity in attempting to trace all the principal characteristics of classic architecture to the form of the primitive hut. Thus the shaft of the column is supposed to have had its origin in the upright timbers raised to support the roof, while the plinth at its base, and the abacus of the capital, severally represent the stones that were employed to raise or cover the vertical posts. It is easy to imagine the successive advances from one stage in the art of building to another, from the rude hut to the well-formed cottage; but it is not so to trace the progress of the introduction of ornament, and of those subservient members usually called mouldings. It is probable, however, that the constant observation, if not study, of nature, conduced in a great degree to the progressive development of taste in architecture.

In all the orders of architecture, the column is the principal part, for it so regulates every other part of an edifice that it may almost be said to be the order itself. A column may be divided into three parts: the base, the shaft, and the capital. All columns have not a base, for it is omitted in some of the most beautiful specimens of the Grecian Doric, while on the other hand some are mounted on pedestals, which are also divided into three parts, the plinth, the die, and the cornice. Above the capital of the column is placed the entablature, consisting of an architrave, frieze, and cornice, the first of these being the lowest member. Some of these members consist of two or more mouldings, which differ in size and in proportion according to the order in which they are employed.

Now it must be evident that to obtain a suitable proportion between all these several parts, and to give to every member its proper importance and outline, there must be some standard of measurement permanently and universally adopted. According to the system employed by architects, every portion of an order has a relation to, and is measured from, the lower diameter of the column, which is called a module, except in the Doric, in which a module is half a diameter, or thirty minutes; for the entire diameter is in all cases divided into sixty equal parts, called minutes. The importance of having this standard of measurement cannot be too highly estimated, for if the members and mouldings had no other relation to each other than that which could be given by some general rule, and a system of measurement depending upon the will of an individual, there would be a great difficulty in drawing the orders, and in suiting the dimensions to the place in which the column was to be used.

The first object of the architect is, therefore, to determine the lower diameter of the column, which is to be the scale by which all the other parts are to be constructed. The diameter of columns varies with the height, and columns of different orders have not the same diameters when the heights are equal. There is in fact a proportion in every order, between the height of the column and the lower diameter; and by a knowledge of the relative proportions, the module may be discovered, and the order accurately described.

" In the opinion of Scamozzi," says Sir Wm. Chambers, " columns should not be less than seven of their diameters in height, nor more than ten; the former being, according to him, a good proportion in the Tuscan, and the latter in the Corinthian order. The practice of the ancients in their best works being conformable to this precept, I have, as authorised by the doctrine of Vitruvius, made the Tuscan column seven diameters in height, and the Doric eight; the Ionic nine, as Palladio and Vignola have done, and the Corinthian and Composite ten, which last measure is a mean between the proportions observed in the Parthenon, and at the three columns in the Campo Vaccino, both which are esteemed most excellent models of the Corinthian order.

The height of the entablature, in all the orders, I have made one quarter of the height of the column, which was the common practice of the ancient Romans, who in all sorts of entablatures seldom exceeded, or fell much short of that measure."

A description of the several orders has been given in other parts of this work.

It frequently happens that a person who has resolved to build, and has determined upon the arrangements and plans, is quite unable to inform his builder or architect what style would .be most agreeable to his wishes, either from a want of knowledge, or a fastidious determination not to adopt the first design that is given. In such cases it is necessary to prepare two or three designs for the same plan, and the method of doing this we have attempted to show in the plates to which this description particularly refers. To do this in such manner as to secure the approbation of the proprietor, two geometrical, as well as two perspective views, as in the accompanying plates, should be prepared; for it is only by this means that he will be able to obtain an accurate perception of the appearance that would be presented when the building is erected. The geometrical elevation, however, is of most value to the artificer, and it is for the unpractised eye perspective views are generally prepared.

Plate LXVII.

Figure 1. Is the end elevation of a cottage in the Tudor style of architecture.

Figure 2. Is the end elevation of a cottage in the Grecian Doric style.

Figure 3. Is a ground plan suited to both these elevations, and consists of a front parlour, 22 feet by 16 feet, back parlour, or bed-room, 16 feet square, kitchen 14 feet by 11 feet, with stairs, larder, coal-cellar, water-closet, &c. The parlours are intended to have joists laid on sleepers of the usual scantlings and bearings, and these are to be covered with $1\frac{1}{4}$ inch floor-boards. This floor is intended to be 8 feet 6 inches high. Bed-rooms may be constructed in the roof.

Figure 4. Is an elevation of the tops and bases of the chimneys for the Tudor cottage, showing the method of finishing.

Figure 5. Is a plan of the same.

Plate LXVIII.

Figure 1. Is a perspective view of the Tudor cottage, the elevation of which is given in Figure 1, of Plate LXVII.

Figure 2. Is a plan of the roofs, one half showing the naked timbers and flues, the other half the slating complete.

Figure 3. Is the end elevation of the dormer window, showing also a section of the gutter cornice, rafter, &c.

Figure 4. Is an elevation of the dormer window.

Figure 5. Is a plan of the same.

Plate LXIX.

Figure 1. Is a perspective view of the Grecian Doric cottage, the end elevation of which is given in Figure 2, of Plate LXVII.

Figure 2.—An elevation of part of the turret, which is intended to be the general receiver of the smoke from all the flues. This method has been introduced in several of our designs, and has been described in page 7.

Figure 3.—Elevation of the top of the same turret.

Figure 4.—Cap of Doric column.

Figure 5.—Base of the same.

Figure 6.—Plan of turret, showing the flues before the valves are fixed.

Figure 7.—The cornice of pediment.

Figure 8.—The cap of antæ.

Figure 9.—The balustrade under portico.

Either of these buildings may be erected for about the sum of £275.

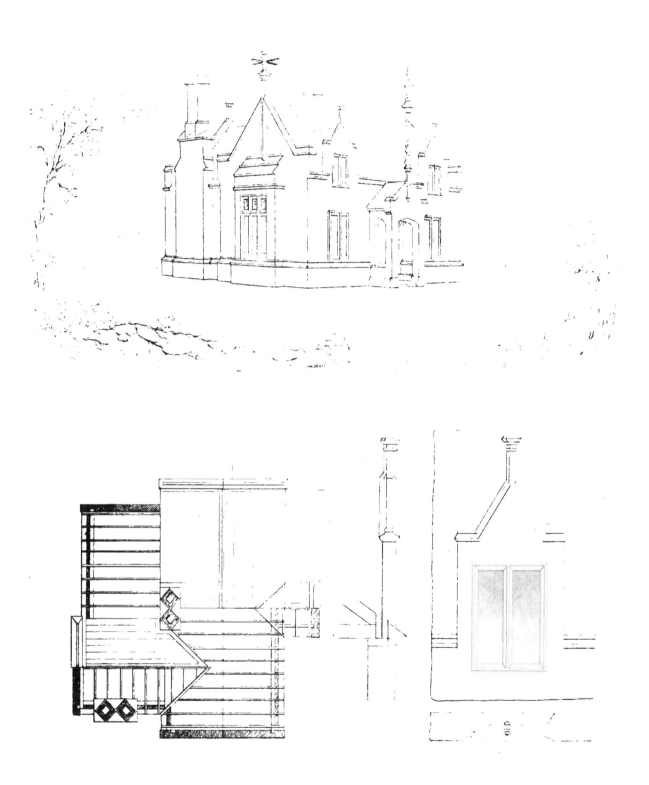

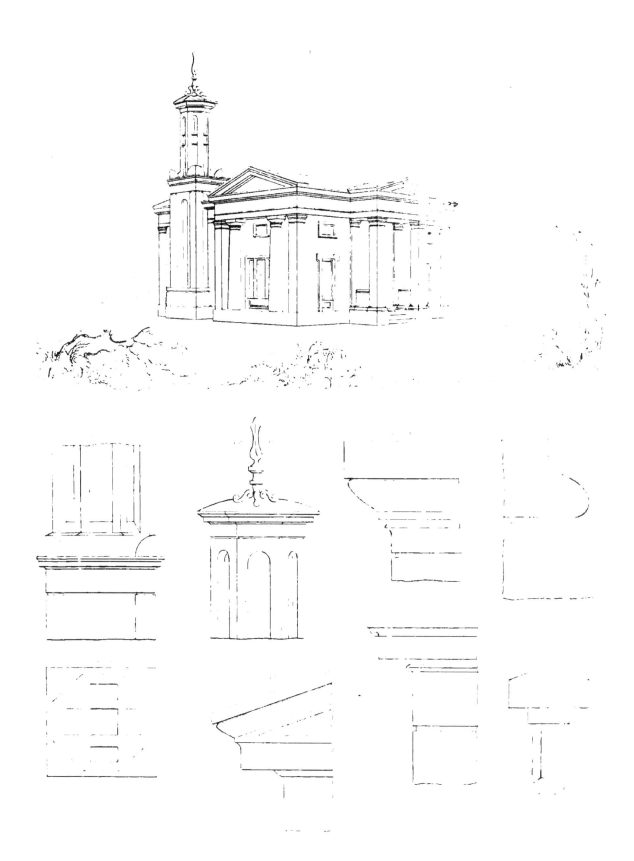

93

It is a singular fact, that until within the last few years, architecture was but little studied or observed by the public, and scarcely considered as one of the fine arts. It was even defined by the authors who wrote upon it, as the art of building. Architecture is the art of building, but it is something more; it is the art of building according to certain general and established rules, by which proportion, elegance, and grace, may be secured. It also includes the art of design. If architecture were nothing more than the science of constructing edifices, every man might boast of possessing it; the wild and uncivilized tribes of Africa, as well as the ancient Egyptians and Greeks. But while the temporary wood or mud hut of the barbarian, proves that man possesses naturally, the ability to erect or build for himself a place of shelter; the splendid temples of Greece and Rome, and the public and private buildings of our own times, equally establish the fact, that man also possesses a capability of improving his natural faculty, and of creating forms of beauty.

Architecture is a study requiring a constant and laborious attention; it is so extensive, and is connected so closely with the interests of all classes of society. An architect must, in the first place, be thoroughly acquainted with the art of construction, and know how to arrange all his materials, so as to support the necessary weights. He must be acquainted theoretically and practically, with the operation of all the trades employed in building, so as to direct the workmen in the best methods of completing his own intentions. The architect must also be acquainted with the wants of every class of society, and provide for the convenience of those who employ him; whether it be an edifice for a dwelling-house, or a manufactory. These are his duties, but he must also possess the capability of designing, so as to give a suitable degree of elegance and character to all his structures. Those who study architecture as an elegant art, and not as a profession, will confine their attention to the rules of proportion, the varieties of style, and the history of the art among different nations, and at different periods.

In designing a building, many things are to be considered; for it must have

2 c

stability, be a pleasant object, and commodious; and there must be a perfect relation between all the parts.

The stability of the building will depend upon having a good foundation, employing proper materials, and having those materials of a sufficient size; strong enough to carry the weights which may be upon them, and not so heavy as to overload the structure.

That the building should be a pleasant object, and agreeable to the view, it must have a character suited to the purpose for which it is to be employed. A prison should be a plain massive structure, and give the spectator an idea of punishment; a palace should be an elegant, decorated, regal edifice; a villa should have an aspect of comfort and retirement. But above all things, the proportion between the several parts must be considered; for how appropriate soever the appearance of the building may be to the purpose for which it may be intended, though the arrangements be perfect, and the design admirable, if the parts be not proportioned to each other, there can be no beauty, and the man of taste will be disgusted instead of being pleased.

There are a few general rules or principles by which the architect should be always governed, and by an acquaintance with which an inexperienced person may fairly criticise any edifice. Every part of a building should be evidently necessary, and intended for a specific purpose. The ornaments should be of a character suited to that of the building. No ornament should be introduced merely for the sake of decoration, and, as it were, independent of the building, but every part should appear so necessary, that the structure would be incomplete without it. These principles apply to all styles of architecture, to the various ages of Gothic as well as to the orders of the Grecian. But while these rules are insisted on, it must not be forgotten, that all styles should represent some character or quality, a truth we have insisted upon in another part of this book.

There are some persons who maintain the foolish idea, that because the

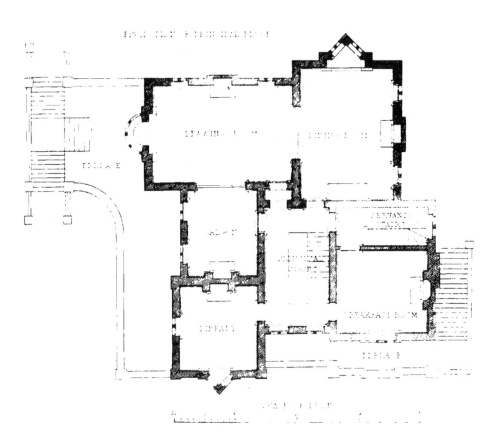

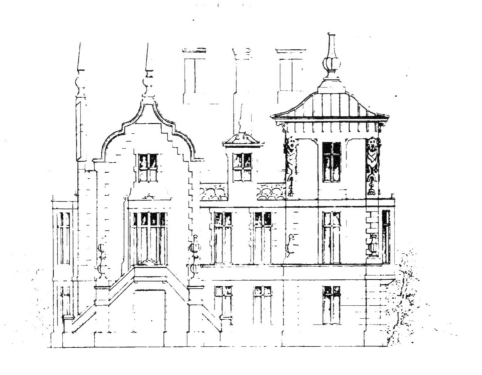

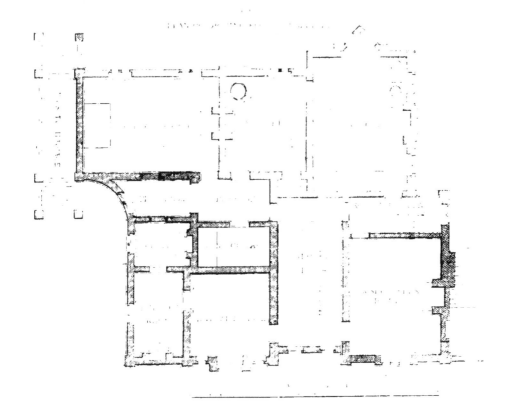

three orders are representatives of qualities, any deviation from them shows a want of taste. Montesquieu says, of the Gothic, that "the ornaments fatigue by their littleness, and are so confused that no part can be distinguished from another; and from their number, there are none upon which the eye can rest, which proves it to be unnatural." A modern professional writer, speaking of the same style, says, "it is a sort of monster, engendered by a chaos of ideas, in the night of barbarity." The reader must be well aware that we do not maintain these opinions, but have rather, we hope, disproved them by our designs.

Plate LXX.

Figure 1. Is the entrance elevation of a design for a villa in the Elizabethan style of architecture.

Figure 2. Is the plan of the principal floor, the access to which, from the pleasure grounds or lawn, is by a double flight of steps, landing on a bold and handsome terrace. This floor consists of a saloon, 14 feet by 12 feet; a drawing room, 23 feet by 14 feet; library or study, 14 feet square; dining-room, 25 feet by 14 feet; breakfast-room, 15 feet by 14 feet; with principal and secondary staircase. This story is 11 feet high.

Plate LXXI.

Figure 1. Is the elevation of one of the sides.

Figure 2. Is the plan of the ground floor or offices, and consists of an entrance hall 14 feet square, and a principal staircase; housekeeper's room, 18 feet by 15 feet; servants' staircase, 15 feet by 7 feet; kitchen 22 feet by 15 feet; scullery 14 feet by 13 feet; servants' hall 22 feet by 15 feet; still room, 10 feet by 7 feet; butler's room, 14 feet by 8 feet; with a plate room and wine cellar. It is proposed to pave the entrance hall, principal and secondary staircase, wine cellar, servants' hall, kitchen, scullery, passage, &c. with stone; the other apartments are to be boarded. This story is intended to be 9 feet 6 inches high.

96

The bed rooms are to be, according to our intentions, on the story over the principal floor, and may be so divided as to suit almost any arrangements that may be considered necessary.

DETAILS.

Plate LXXII.

Figure   1.—Section of water-tabling on gable ends, &c.

Figure   2.—Section of string course.

Figure   3.—Scroll and cornice for dormer windows.

Figure   4.—Elevation of one of the consoles under eaves.

Figure   5.—Side elevation of the same.

Figure   6.—Elevation of one of the finials.

Figure   7.—Coping for terrace.

Figure   8.—Elevation of chimney shafts.

Figure   9.—Section of smaller chimney.

Figure 10.—Elevation of pedestal to principal terrace.

Figure 11.—Moulding for architrave.

Figure 12.—Section of sliding door with architrave, linings, &c.

Figure 13.—Elevation of pedestal for principal stairs, &c.

Figure 14.—Cap of pedestal to a large scale.

Figure 15.—Cap of hand-rail.

Figure 16.—Skirting for principal rooms.

Figure 17.—Plan of folding doors, showing also the method of suspending them.

It is calculated that this building may be executed for the sum of £2800.

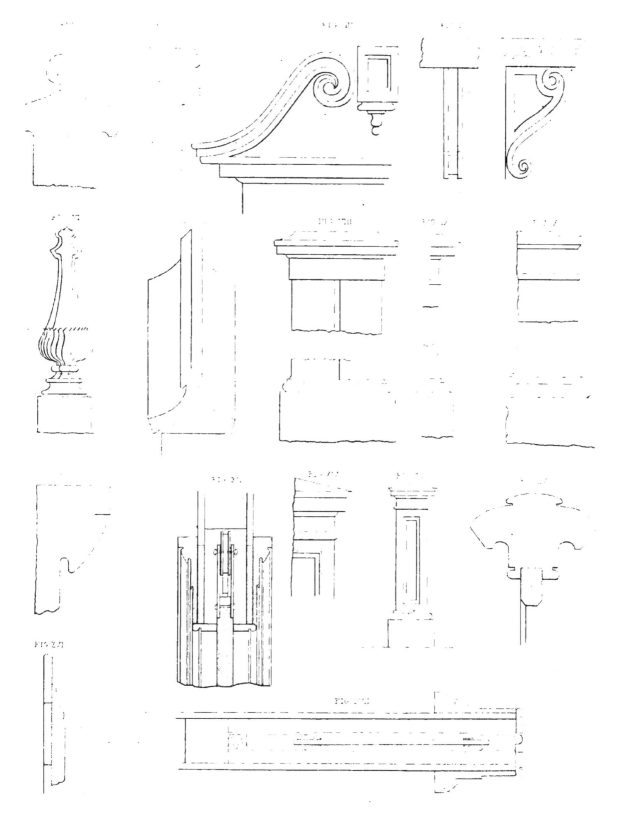

97

In the selection of that style of architecture best suited to a particular situation, a good judgment and an improved taste are absolutely necessary. The design which may be admirably adapted for one situation may be altogether unfit for another, however appropriate it may be for the uses to which the building is to be applied. Although this fact is seldom acknowledged as a principle, and rarely understood by builders in the abstract statement, its truth may be demonstrated by a candid analysis of the styles adopted by those nations who have made any advance in the science of architecture. We are accustomed to designate the various peculiarities as though they were different orders, and to give them the names of those countries in which they are supposed to have had their origin or rise. A person ignorant of the art might be thus led into error, and suppose that the style was only applicable to the country whose name it takes; but with the same propriety it might be imagined, that over the entire extent of any political division of the earth's surface there must necessarily be the same temperature, physical peculiarities, and natural adaptations. We might give many illustrations, were this necessary, of the use of styles of architecture almost opposite in their general characteristics, within the circuit of a few miles, each being well adapted to the locality in which the building is placed. There is generally as little similarity between the architecture of mountainous and lowland countries, as those of cold and hot climates. If there be a style having any claim to be considered universal, it is that which is called the classical, which includes not only the Grecian and Roman orders, but all that class of buildings in which the main lines are horizontal.

We may here be permitted to make a few remarks upon the method of preparing working drawings, such as will assist the country builder, who from any cause may be required to execute our designs without the assistance of a professional man.

Working drawings for small buildings, whether plans or sections, should be drawn to the scale of one quarter of an inch to a foot, not only because the size is sufficiently large to allow the draughtsman to figure every portion accurately and fully, but also because it gives the artisan an opportunity of measuring every part with his rule as he proceeds.

When the elevations, plans, and sections, are thus prepared, the working-drawings for all the mouldings, cornices, strings, and projections of every kind, should be finished, and these must be either a quarter, half, or full size. The greatest possible care must be taken in designing and completing these, not only to preserve the intended proportions, but also to so form the several parts that they may all appear necessary to complete the whole, and be in character one with another.

Before the building is commenced, the aspect, which is of the greatest importance, should be carefully considered. Every one is aware of the necessity of this in providing for the comfort and enjoyment of a family in our changeable climate; or a few months residence in apartments having a northern aspect would soon give practical information. But there is another reason for this consideration. For a considerable portion of the year it is necessary that we should have a means of heating our dwellings, and the prejudices of the country are in favour of open fire-places and warming by radiation. The construction and situation of these flues are, therefore, of great moment; that the smoke may pass away freely, and the inhabitants be secured from the great but common nuisance of a smoky house. In those places where the principle already described is adopted, the builder must endeavour to ascertain from what quarter of the heavens the winds most frequently and furiously blow, and so dispose the rooms in which fires will be most often required, that they may be in the least possible degree affected by them. This is too frequently neglected by both architects and builders; and to the indifference they feel may be attributed the occurrence of smoky chimneys, and the difficulty afterwards experienced in every attempt to remedy the evil.

The plan of drainage is another important consideration for the builder, but this he will be almost sure to investigate carefully. After a survey of the spot

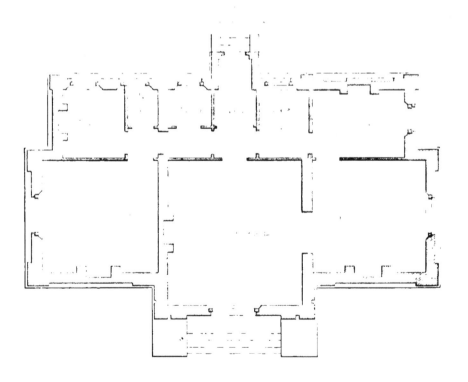

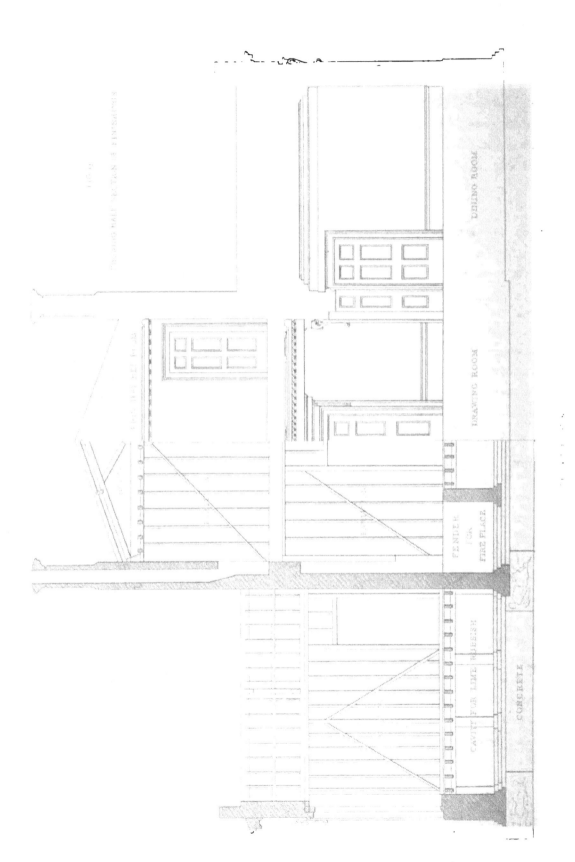

chosen as the site of the building, and the several levels being taken, a plan should be prepared to a quarter scale to direct the workmen: the method of preparing these drawings will be explained with sufficient examples in another part of this work.

Plate LXXIII.

The design represented in Fig. 1 is one of the description termed classical, and is suited for any situation where a villa may be erected with propriety. .The perspective view shows the principal or lawn front, and the side elevation.

Figure 2. Is the ground plan of the building. Supposing the building to have been erected, a visitor, after passing the entrance-porch, would come into a small hall which leads into the drawing-room, breakfast-room, .study, and library. The dining-room is approached through the library or drawing-room. · The kitchen and domestic offices are supposed in this design to be beneath the ground-floor; but in situations where the space of ground covered is not an object of importance, it would be found more convenient to have them on the same level, although a slight alteration in the arrangement of the ground-floor would then be necessary. If the design be erected for a small family, that portion of, the building appropriated in the plan to the breakfast-room and study might be converted into a kitchen and scullery, or larder.

Plate LXXIV.

Figure 1. Exhibits a half section of the method of construction, supposed to be taken through the breakfast and drawing-rooms in the line A B, and shows the construction of the partition separating them from the study and hall, of the concrete, footing, and flooring, of the principal walls and roof, as well as the partitions and roof of the main or central portion of the structure.

100

Figure 2. Is the half section of the finishings. The scantlings of the several timbers cannot be shown in drawings of such a scale, and cannot be given conveniently in this work; these practical details must be left with the builder, or more properly with the architect who has the superintendence of the works.

Plate LXXV.

Shows the plan of the building in various stages, and the method of construction.

Figure 1. Is a quarter plan, showing the concrete foundation and footings. The proportions best suited for concrete are two parts of gravel, one of sand, and one-ninth of ground lime. These should be thoroughly mixed together, and thrown into the trenches from as great a height as possible, so that by the fall the entire mass may be made more compact. Concrete is now very commonly employed by architects and builders to form a good solid foundation; it need not, however, be introduced in small buildings when the natural foundation is firm.

Figure 2. Is a quarter plan, showing the method of bedding the sleepers on the brick piers to carry the joists.

Figure 3. Is a quarter plan, showing the floor-joists and trimmer; in fact, the plan of the naked flooring.

Figure 4. Is a quarter plan, showing the finishings of all the work. Here we have the floor-boards laid, the windows fixed in the openings with their backs and linings, the landing and steps laid upon the brick arch turned to support them, the walls plastered, and all completed for the use of the occupier.

It is estimated that this building may be executed for about the sum of £675, the price varying in different situations according to the price of materials, the distance of carriage, the value of labour, and the difficulties or facilities which may be given to the execution of the work.

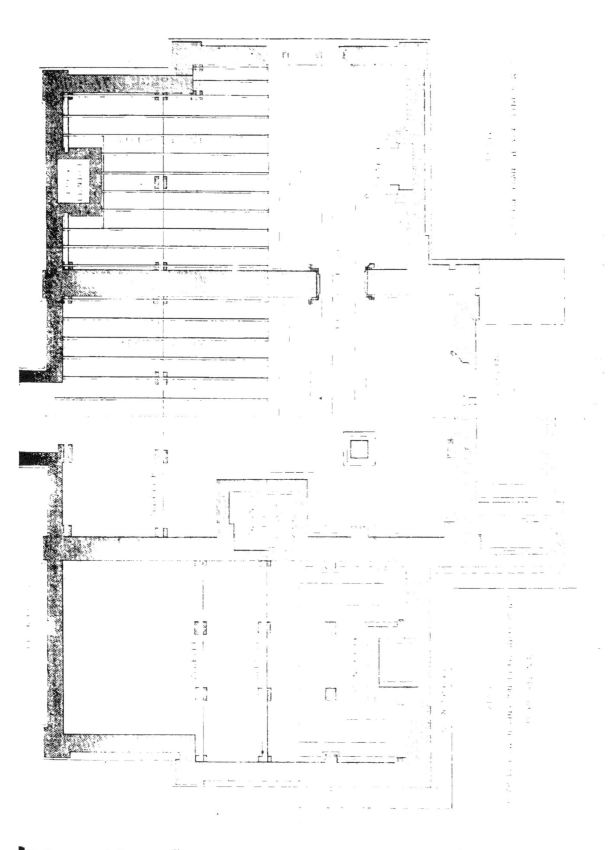

We have sometimes heard persons complain that architecture is, both as an art and as a science, of most limited extent, because it is founded on certain abstract rules which cannot be invaded. From this assertion they have deduced that the judgment is cramped and the imagination held in leading strings. With the same propriety it might be said that painting is a feeble and inefficient art, because there are only seven rays in the spectrum, and one of these, or some modification of one or more, must be employed by the artist; or that sculpture is a mere work of imitation, because its noblest effort is in faithfully copying the productions of nature; or, as we would rather express the same idea, in giving to an unshaped mass of stone the attitudes, proportions, and apparent passions with which God has invested his living creatures. What would be the amount of ridicule reserved for that man who should assert that an art was without rules, or that the proportions between the parts of any created thing could be changed without offending the eye and destroying the harmony of the design established by the Creator? In the animal world we observe all the varieties of form between the light and elegant grace of the stag, and the unwieldy cumbersomeness of the thick-skinned animals; the elastic movement of the undulating snake, and the awkward retrograde motion of the crab. But who will say that the form or motion is not as admirable in one creature as in another, or that the Creator has not fully exhibited his skill in the construction of all? We sometimes indulge our hasty judgments by condemning a creature as ugly or deformed, and compare it with another we call beautiful. Were we to examine more closely we should discover that each was created for an especial end, and that the form and motion are suited to the character and condition. If then no general standard of beauty can be discovered in nature, if all excellence depends on the fitness of forms, habits and sensibilities, to the wants and conditions of the creatures, how important must it be that in all works of art, which are more or less adaptations of nature, and representations of human feelings and passions, we should be governed by those laws which are founded on the fitness of things to a proposed end.

There are five orders of architecture in that style denominated classical, and the usual opinion is, that a modern architect when designing in either of these has nothing more to do than to follow without reserve all the proportions adopted by the ancients, "when, in fact," to use the words of a modern author, " his duty is to explore the treasures with which the vestiges of antiquity and the best works abound, viewing them not as documents and patterns merely, but as invaluable manifestations of mind, in which may be read the very thoughts of their authors, and where may be found the reasonings upon which they acted ; thence deducing principles and rules for controlling and directing those exuberances of fancy, with which he who hopes to become a great architect should be gifted."

It has been often said with a sneer of contempt, that it is very strange modern architects cannot discover a new order, or that they should be satisfied, even in the present day, with following the practice of the ancient Greeks and Romans. With as much propriety it might be said that it is very strange philosophers have not discovered new rays in the solar spectrum since the days of Newton, whereas they have, in fact, discovered that the primitive rays are but three instead of seven. The Doric order is the representation of strength and masculine boldness, the Corinthian of delicacy and elegance. These may be said to be the two primitive orders, and the Ionic is the intermediate. The Tuscan is a heavy modification of the Doric, and the Composite a variety of the Corinthian.

But although we cannot ever hope to add a new order, yet it is possible to invent a new style ; and hence have arisen all those splendid varieties of architecture which are used in modern times. Belonging to the same genus as the Grecian and Roman, if we may so express ourselves, are the Italian and Swiss. The Gothic is altogether different in its character, but may be classed with the Moorish, Old English, and other styles, in which pointed arches are introduced, pinnacles, turrets, and ornamented gables.

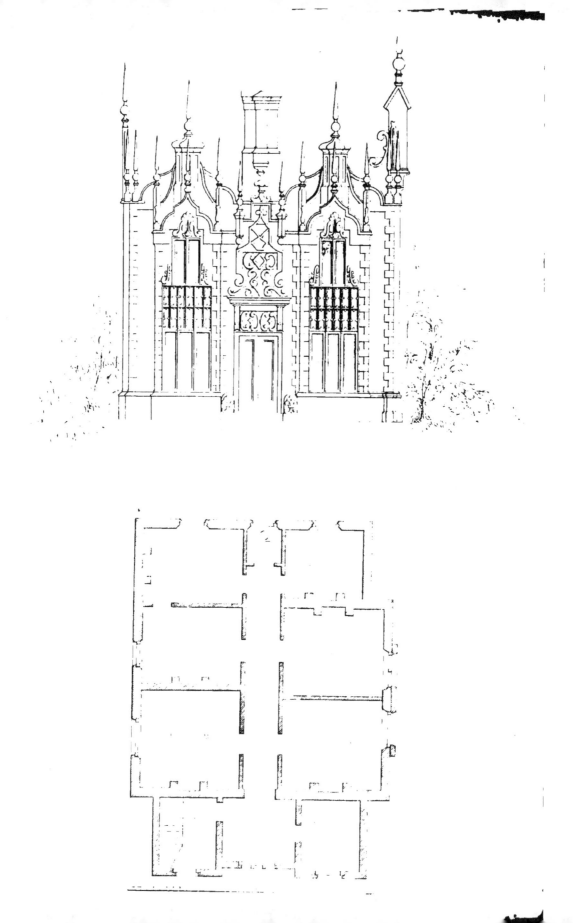

In Plate LXXVI. we have introduced a design in the Elizabethan style of architecture, which is a modification of the Gothic. The decorations are both numerous and rich, and would therefore be expensive if they were carved in stone. But in such a cottage as we have designed, it will be sufficient if they are executed in some hard wood, such as chestnut, which is peculiarly well adapted for the purpose.

In selecting a spot for an Elizabethan cottage, more care and judgment is required than for almost any other style of architecture. Its rich decorations and the pointed character of all the details, require a similarity of scene. Were a novice to erect our design on an open lawn, forming a part of a widely extended plain of cultivated fields, with only here and there a tree rising to a height greater than the hedges or stone walls, which form the divisions of property, we wonder how great would be his disappointment, and what the amount of ridicule that he would bear! The cottage is one suited to a far different scene, one which is not only well-wooded, but with trees of a particular form. It would assort well with the fir and the poplar, with here and there an umbrant chestnut, and a wide-spreading luxuriant oak. If erected in a suitable situation, and according to the plans we present to the reader, the cottage would be well adapted for a respectable family, with a small establishment.

Plate LXXVI.

Figure 1. Is a geometrical elevation of the entrance front of a design in the Elizabethan style of architecture. The dotted lines show the basement floor, should it be necessary to introduce the domestic offices below the ground, which should always be avoided if possible.

Figure 2. Is the chamber plan, which consists of six bed-rooms and two dressing-rooms, with store-closet and water-closet.

Plate LXXVII.

Figure 1. Shows the side elevation of the building.

Figure 2. Shows the ground plan, which consists of an entrance hall, 10 feet by 10 feet, breakfast-room, 15 feet by 15 feet, dining-room, 24 feet by 15 feet, drawing-room, 27 feet by 16 feet, and study, 12 feet by 12 feet, with suitable conservatory, staircase, passage, and water-closet. The height of this story from the floor to the ceiling should be 15 feet.

DETAILS.

Plate LXXVIII.

Figure 1.—The coping and finial.

Figure 2.—The elevation of the same.

Figure 3.—The elevation of the chimney top.

Figure 4.—The base of the same.

Figure 5.—A plan of the flues.

Figure 6.—A plan of the finial and coping.

Figure 7.—The external elevation of one-half of the entrance door.

Figure 8.—The internal elevation of one-half of the same door.

Figure 9.—The section of entrance door.

This design may be executed for about £1250 ; but the cost will, of course, vary in different situations according to the value of materials and labour, and the difficulties or facilities which may arise from particular sites.

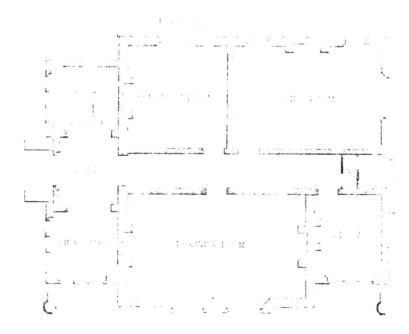

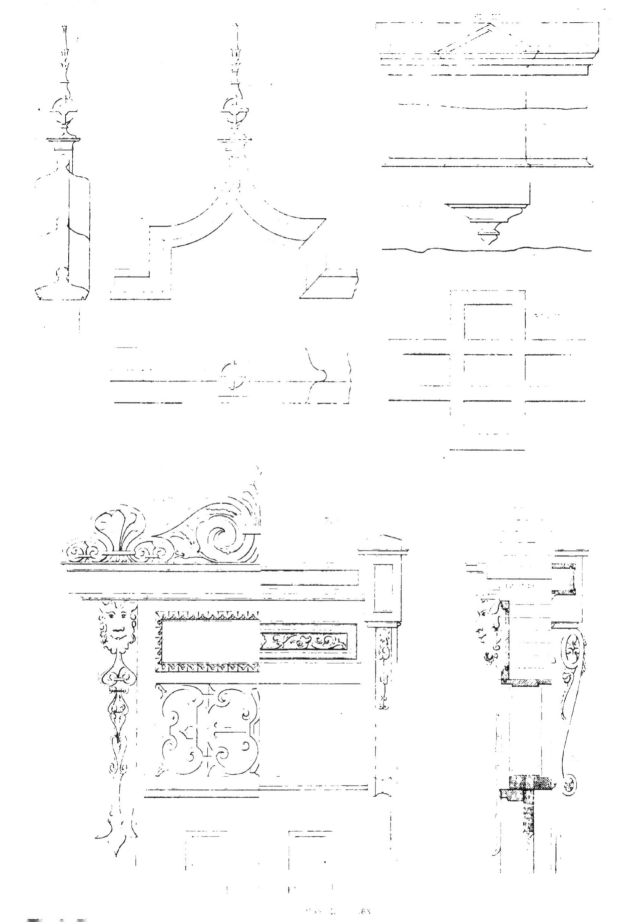

105

That style of architecture falsely called Gothic, from an erroneous opinion as to its origin, is in all its varieties pleasing to the man of taste, and has an imposing effect upon every observer. As we have introduced it in several of our designs, it may not be uninteresting to the reader if we give, in this place, a general abstract of some of the opinions which have been maintained by writers who have endeavoured to trace its origin.

The first hypothesis to which we shall refer, is that in which the style is said to be a corruption of the Roman, introduced by the Italian architects of the middle ages. Guided by this opinion, one author speaks of the church and palace of St. Mark at Venice, as an admirable example of the depraved style of architecture at the period when they were erected; while another desires to name it Romanesque, as pointing out the derivation of this " vicious and barbarous deviation from classic taste."

Another class of writers have adopted the opinion proposed by Sir Christopher Wren, that Gothic architecture was derived from the Saracens. In consequence of the Crusades, according to the statements of these authors, it was brought into Europe, adopted in ecclesiastical structures, and daily improved upon by those who superintended their construction. To this it has been objected, that the churches built subsequently to the Crusades do not exhibit a single feature of the Saracenic architecture.

Other persons trace the origin of Gothic architecture, to observations on the effect produced by the intersection of semi-circular arches, not at all uncommon in Saxon and Norman buildings. This theory was stated by Dr. Bentham, and afterwards warmly supported by Dr. Milner, and has in the present day many advocates.

Dr. Warburton entertained the fanciful idea, that when the Goths conquered Spain they struck out a new species of architecture for themselves, which in fact was the Gothic; for, having professed paganism and worshipped the Deity in groves, they were anxious to imitate them as nearly as possible in their sacred edifices. To this theory Lord Orford very justly objects: "The Gothic style seems to bespeak an amplification of the minute, not a diminution of the great. Warburton's groves are nonsense; it was not a passage from barbarism to art, but from one species of the art to another."

These are some of the principal theories which have been maintained, and we leave the reader to determine which he will adopt as the most probable. For each he will find a large body of evidence; and may, perhaps, if uninfluenced by any previous prejudice, have some difficulty in balancing probabilities. Considering the very general use of the style for almost all classes of buildings, it is by no means an uninteresting or unimportant investigation. We do not advocate the introduction of questions purely speculative; but when hypotheses require deep investigation, they frequently induce a minute inquiry, and often lead us near to an approximate estimate of the capability of acquiring truth, if not to the discovery of truth itself.

In another part of this work we have attempted to show that Gothic architecture presented very distinctive characters at different periods. There is one style in which the ornaments are few and not rich in design; there is another in which the ornaments are of the most elaborate character, decorated with pinnacles, flowing tracery, and a profusion of carving: an intermediate style connects the extremes. Neither of these, however, is suited to domestic architecture generally, although there are a few instances in which the situation and the extent of the structure offer favourable opportunities for the display of a judicious design.

The style adopted in Plate LXXIX. is better adapted for villa architecture than any other with which we are acquainted, and we have endeavoured to show its capability in this design. From these general remarks it is now necessary to turn, and explain the advantages of the situation in which we have placed our Gothic cottage, and the plan of its construction.

There is, perhaps, no object in nature so interesting as water in a land-

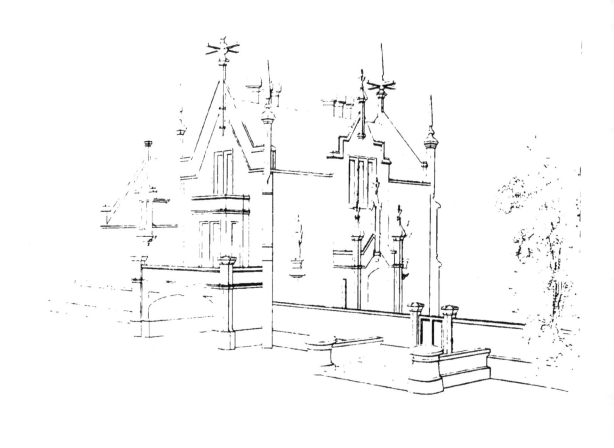

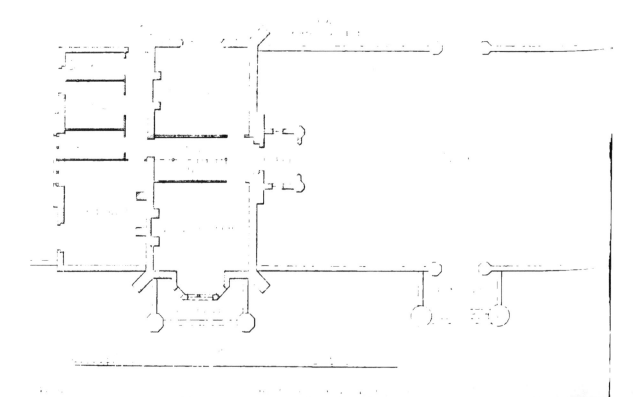

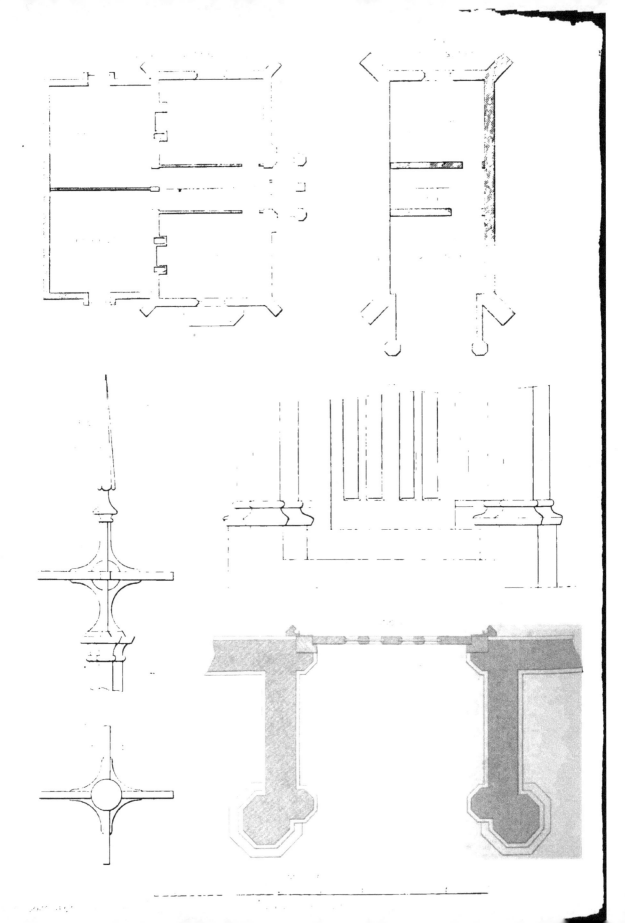

scape. Under all its varying features it attracts attention, and gives a peculiar character to the situation in which it is found. When its surface is smooth and unruffled, lighted up by the morning, mid-day, or evening sun, it gives a reflected beauty to the entire scene; and when in a state of most violent agitation it imparts a grandeur equally impressive to every lover of nature. We have heard that some persons dislike music, but we have never heard of a person who was displeased with a view of water in a landscape. The richest blossoms and flowers fade away, and the trees of the forest are stripped of their luxuriant foliage, but both in winter and in summer water is pleasing. To these circumstances we may probably attribute the frequent erection of villas either on the banks or in the immediate vicinity of lakes or rivers. The design represented in Plate LXXIX. is admirably adapted for such situations.

Plate LXXIX.

Figure 1. Is a perspective view of a cottage, or fishing-box, in the Gothic style of architecture, to be built on the margin of a river or some other body of water.

Figure 2. Is the ground plan, consisting of an entrance porch, a dining-room 16 feet by 13 feet, drawing-room 18 feet by 16 feet, kitchen 16 feet by 12 feet, larder 9 feet by 6 feet, a water-closet of the same dimensions, and a store-room 9 feet square. It is proposed to board the principal rooms, and pave the offices with stone.

Plate LXXX.

Figure 1. Is a plan of the basement, consisting of a boat-house 25 feet by 15 feet, cellar 15 feet by 12 feet, with a stair-case to ground-floor.

Figure 2. Is a plan of the chamber-floor, and consists of four good bed-rooms.

108

Figure 3. Is an elevation showing a new method of fixing a zinc finial.

Figure 4. Is a plan of the same.

Figure 5. Is a plan showing the stone-work of the entrance-porch and door.

Figure 6. Is an elevation of the bottom of the porch, showing the steps and bottom of turrets and door.

DETAILS.

Plate LXXXI.

Figure 1.—A plan of the angular buttress.

Figure 2.—An elevation of the same.

Figure 3.—The top of metal finial, showing the method of fixing.

Figure 4.—A section of the angular buttress, taken on the line A B on plan, and showing the profile of the decrease.

Figure 5.—The front elevation of coping to the gable end.

Figure 6.—The end elevation of the same.

Figure 7.—The plan of the same.

Figure 8.—The capping to wall of terrace.

This design may be executed according to the drawing for the sum of about £520.

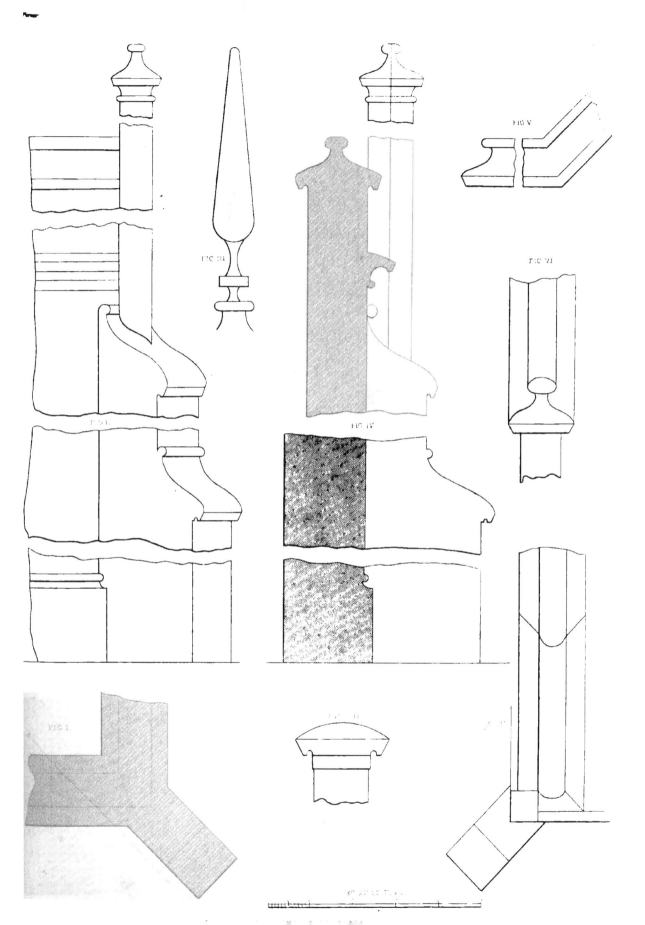

FIG V

FIG VI

FIG III

FIG II

FIG IV

FIG I

SCALE OF FEET

109

Among the various kinds of materials employed in the erection of buildings, none are more common, or more useful, than bricks. There are many places on the surface of the earth, where men have fixed their residence, that are not only destitute of mineral substances fit for use as building materials, but also so far distant from any place where they can be obtained, that wood only could have been employed in building if bricks had not been invented. The importance of the art of brickmaking is, therefore, most evident, for many large and important districts would otherwise have been altogether unfit for the residence of large communities of men. The art of brickmaking is of great antiquity, for in the earliest ages of the world it was practised, and many of the manufactures of an ancient date remain to our own day, and are collected by the curious. In the book "Genesis," an account is given of the agreement between the descendants of those who had escaped from an almost universal catastrophe, to travel into the land of Shinar, better known to the moderns as Chaldea, for the purpose of making bricks. "And they said one to another, Go to, let us make bricks, and burn them thoroughly. And they had brick for stone, and slime had they for mortar." In the first book of Herodotus, a celebrated Grecian historian, this interesting passage is alluded to. The resolve was carried into execution, and that tower was built, known from all others by the result—the confusion of tongue or language.

In the same sacred authority we are informed that when the Hebrews had become a great nation in Egypt, and there was then, probably, a fear excited that they would soon be too powerful to submit to the control of the national government, but would rather aim at the usurpation of authority, and seize upon the country, a system of oppression and slavery was adopted. "And the Egyptians made the children of Israel to serve with rigour : and they made their lives bitter with hard bondage, in mortar and in brick, and in all manner of service in the field : all their service, wherein they made them serve, was with rigour."

From these two instances of the manufacture and use of bricks in the earliest ages of the habitable world, and recorded in a book, pamphlet, or tract, the most ancient that has descended to our own times, (if we except the book of Job, which, in the opinion of some scholars, is of still more ancient date,) we feel confident that the art was well known many thousand years ago, and was probably understood among many people whose descendants have degenerated into a most pitiable state of barbarism.

The excavations which have been carried on in the site of ancient Babylon, have disinterred an immense mass of rubbish and brick, and among them also a number of cylinders formed of the hardest stones, and curiously engraven; upon which the learned are much divided in opinion.

From the evidence already given it is quite certain that bricks were used in the construction of buildings in the earliest ages of the world; as soon, indeed, as men congregated together and built cities. But it is still a question of doubt, whether these bricks were burnt or merely dried in the sun. We are well assured both from history and the specimens which remain to our own day, that unburnt bricks were used, but this does not prove that the practice of burning was unknown. Other writers have assumed the opposite conclusion, and from want of evidence, boldly assert that " the burning of bricks was a practice unknown in the earliest ages, and reserved for a more advanced state of the art of building."

In the use of bricks there are both advantages and disadvantages. Being of a more porous texture than most building stones, they unite better with the cement, and being of smaller size, may be carried about with greater ease to any height, and without tackle; but on the other hand, mouldings cannot be carved on them. In the manufacture of bricks, much care is required, and an attention to times. The earth should be dug in the autumn, and be allowed to remain the whole winter exposed to the frost and all the atmospheric changes, which have a tendency to divide the particles. In the spring it should be broken up and softened with water. The next operation is that of tempering, which is usually effected by a mill. This process is not only the most laborious, but the most important, for upon it depends the character

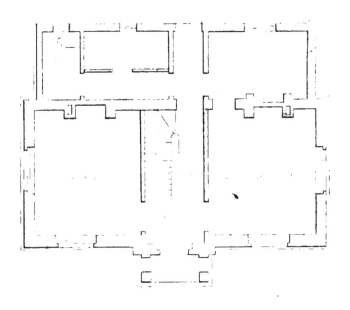

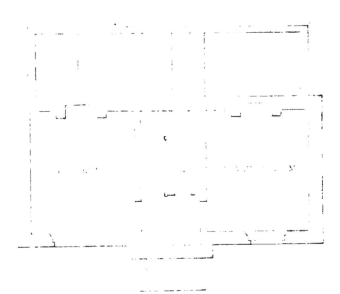

of the brick in a great degree. The clay being thus prepared and brought into a perfectly plastic state, is carried to the bench of the moulder, where the bricks are formed. When the bricks are, by exposure to the air, sufficiently hard to be handled, they are carried to the kiln or clamp, and burnt.

Plate LXXXII.

Figure 1. Is a perspective view of a cottage, which has been designed in the classic style, without the introduction of any ornament, and with the overhanging roof so characteristic of the cottage architecture suited to our climate. This design is one of an unpretending character, but one suited to the wishes and condition of a large number of that class of persons who retire from bustling cities, to spend the remnant of their lives in the quiet of country scenes. We do not, therefore, make any apology for the introduction of this design, and especially as we have given several details which cannot fail to be of use; and to those builders in particular, who are accustomed to the demand for this style and class of cottages.

Figure 2. Is the ground plan of the building, consisting of an entrance porch; a dining room 16 feet by 13 feet; a drawing-room of the same dimensions; a study, 12 feet by 9 feet; and a store room, 9 feet by 7 feet. The height of this story should be about 9 feet 6 inches.

Plate LXXXIII.

Figure 1. Is a plan of the chamber floor, which consists of two large bed-rooms and a dressing-room.

Figure 2. Is the plan of the basement, showing also the foundations of the secondary rooms on the ground floor. These walls may, if more room be required on the basement, be brought down to the same level as the principal buildings. This would give excellent cellars, a scullery, and other convenient domestic offices. In the plan, however, as it is drawn, there are only two rooms; and a closet or larder under the stairs.

D E T A I L S.

Plate LXXXIV.

Figure 1. Exhibits a new method of fixing the common rafters to the pole plate, and forming the cottage eave, cornice, gutter, &c.

Figure 2.—Moulding of string course.

Figure 3.—Cap of antæ of porch.

Figure 4.—Cap of chimney.

Figure 5.—Section of large cornice to portico.

Figure 6.—Section of base of antæ.

Figure 7.—Plan of one of the chamber windows. A. A. Stone jambs. B. B. Mullion. C. C. Metal casements. D. D. Brick jambs.

Figure 8.—Elevation of the same window.

Figure 9.—Section of the window; to the several parts of which the same letters are used as in figure 9.

Figure 10.—Section of cast metal bar, full size.

This cottage may be erected for the sum of about £780.

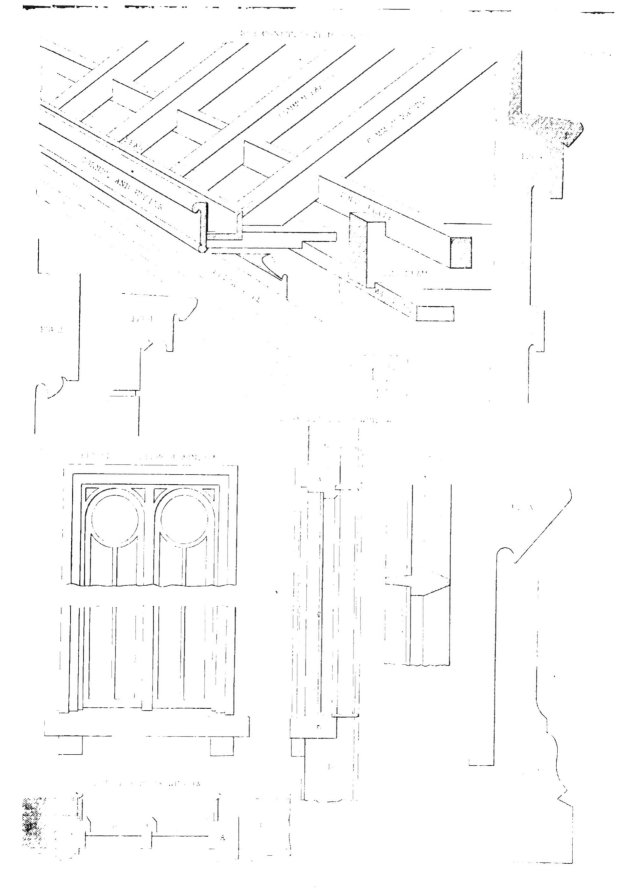

In the early ages of the world men lived in caverns of the earth, or under the shadow of luxuriant vegetation in the depths of the forest; such at least is the opinion usually adopted by the writers who attempt to trace the history of architecture from its rise. This supposition, as must be evident to every reader, is founded upon the hypothesis,—which might be fairly combated—that man, when first placed upon the earth, was left without any intuitive knowledge to the dictates of an improvable reason, and was thus compelled by the necessities of his nature, to form his own habits and to provide for his own comfort and support. Without entering into the debatable question of the extent of man's knowledge, independent of experience, we may at least assume, that being created with faculties capable of indefinite improvement, both by the experience of others and personal investigation, he was left almost entirely to his own resources, and that the early styles of building were of the most simple character.

When the human race increased in number and spread over a large tract of country, differences of habits, opinions, and employments, would necessarily be produced, causing the varieties which we now distinguish as national characters. These have been, no doubt, promoted, if not created, by the localities in which the several sections of mankind happened to settle, and the manner of life in which they indulged before they found a home. One tribe, perhaps, having discovered a suitable place of residence after only a few days' journey, would at once direct its attention to agricultural pursuits, and find a temporary abode not unsuited to the wants and condition of the people, in caverns and forests. The quiet habits of the settlers, however, and the improvement produced in their social condition, would soon lead them to the erection of mud huts and rude edifices of timber. Another tribe may have wandered so far without finding a situation suited to its wishes as a permanent residence, that by a continued nomadic course of life the individuals may have acquired so great a love of rambling as to be indisposed for a more quiet condition, or the steady pursuit of any ordinary vocation. Or we may suppose the tribe to be led by a man of ambitious and daring mind, one who found all his delights in dangers and a continued change of scene. In either instance the dwellings to be adopted must be of a different character to those of the tribes who selected some locality as a permanent residence. The necessity of a defence from the inclemency of the weather, and from the attack of wild animals, must have been observed by all men; but while one tribe, from its habits, was induced to build permanent huts, others would erect tents which were easily formed, and as easily removed or destroyed. In tracing the history of architecture, therefore, we must not attempt to gather our information from those nations which have had no settled home, but from the agricultural and pastoral people, whose interests and prosperity grew with the advances in the art of building.

Let us now suppose a people who have just advanced to that stage of knowledge which has suggested the use of a soft clay in the erection of the external walls of a hut. The choice of clay for this purpose we do not suppose to have been fortuitous, but the result of observation. In all countries there are certain portions of the year in which rain is more abundant than at other periods, and during these wet seasons the clay is made plastic. The returning sun converts the moisture into a vapour, and leaves the clay dry and hard, sufficiently so to resist a considerable pressure. This probably led to the use of clay as a building material, which was either used when softened by the rains, or was rendered plastic by the artificial admixture of water. The heat of the sun being, in oriental countries, powerful and continuous, soon converted the soft and pliable mass of vertical clay into a hard and compact mass, capable of resisting great forces, and but little liable, from its position, to any future influence of the atmosphere.

The next advance in the art of building was the invention of bricks, an easy and natural deduction from the information already acquired. The difficulty of erecting a perpendicular wall of a soft and pliable material, which was to be hardened in the sun, would surely suggest to some ingenious, but inexperienced, and consequently perplexed workman, the advantage of hardening his clay before it was used. We may easily imagine the alacrity with which

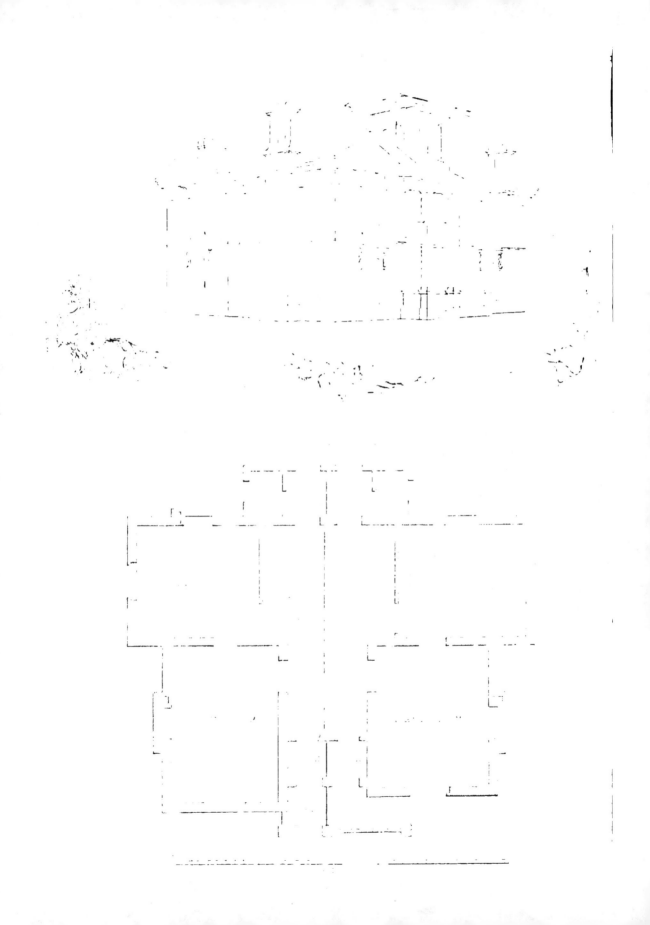

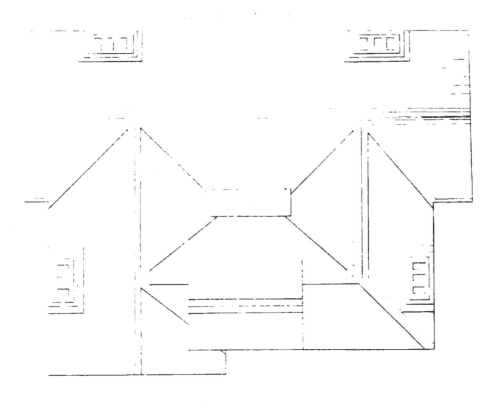

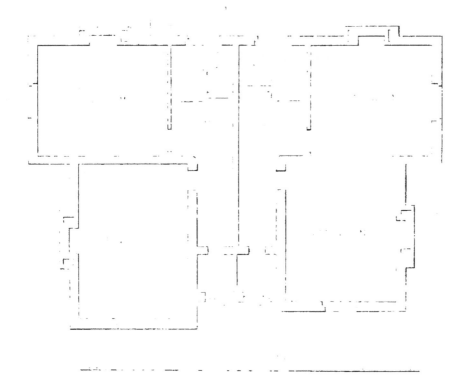

a man would fashion his clay to the shapes required as soon as this thought crossed his mind, and the anxiety with which he would watch the several masses drying in the rays of the vertical sun. To connect these artificial stones would require a further stretch of ingenuity. Clay was, in all probability, first employed for this purpose; for the invention of mortar must have been the result of a continued course of trials, or an accidental discovery when the art of building with dried clay was common. The fashion or form of these bricks, for such the dried masses of clay were, probably changed with the advance of knowledge upon the art of building, until at last they assumed regular forms and were made in moulds.

The discovery and use of building-stones was the next advance in the art. In some situations these hard and compact masses were found upon the surface, and, as it were, offered themselves to the use of man; while in others, they may have been discovered when digging for clay.

In this way we may imagine men to have advanced from one improvement to another, until at last the marble temples of the Greeks were erected over the caverns of their forefathers. By a similar process of reasoning we might, did our space admit, trace the various alterations in the style and arrangement of both domestic and ecclesiastical structures, but we must now proceed to an explanation of the design we have to present to our readers.

Plate LXXXV.

Figure 1. Is a perspective view of a double cottage in a style of architecture combining the Grecian and Italian.

Figure 2. Is the ground plan.

Each cottage contains a kitchen, back kitchen, larder, and other offices on the basement story; parlour and drawing-room on the ground floor; and two bed-rooms on the one pair.

Plate LXXXVI.

Figure 1.—Plan of the roofs, showing the hips, valleys, ridges, &c.

Figure 2.—Plan of the chamber floor

116

DETAILS.

Plate LXXXVII.

Figure 1.—Elevation of a portion of the entrance-door.   A. The door.   B. The base of the pilaster.   C C. The steps.

Figure 2. Plan of the door-frame, door, and linings.   A. The door-frame. B. The door. C. Inside linings. D. Grounds.   E. Architrave. F. Cement jambs, and pilaster.

Figure 3.—Section of the door-head.   The letters of reference in this drawing describe the same parts as in Figure 2, but two others are added.   G. Lintel.   H. Brickwork.

Figure 4.—Section of bottom portion of door.

Figure 5.—Section of principal cornice.   A. Stone core.   B. Brickwork.   C. Cement.

Figure 6.—Base of small antæ.

Figure 7.—Cap of large antæ.

Figure 8.—Cap of chimney.

Figure 9.—Base of antæ.

Figure 10.—Architrave round windows.

Figure 11.—Small cornice over window-heads.   A. Stone core.   B. Brickwork.   C. Cement.

Figure 12.—Cornice for principal rooms.

Figure 13.—Plan of the same.

Figure 14.—Skirting for principal rooms.

Figure 15.—Plan of finishing the internal doors.

Figure 16.—Elevation of the same.

This double cottage may be completed for about the sum of £900.

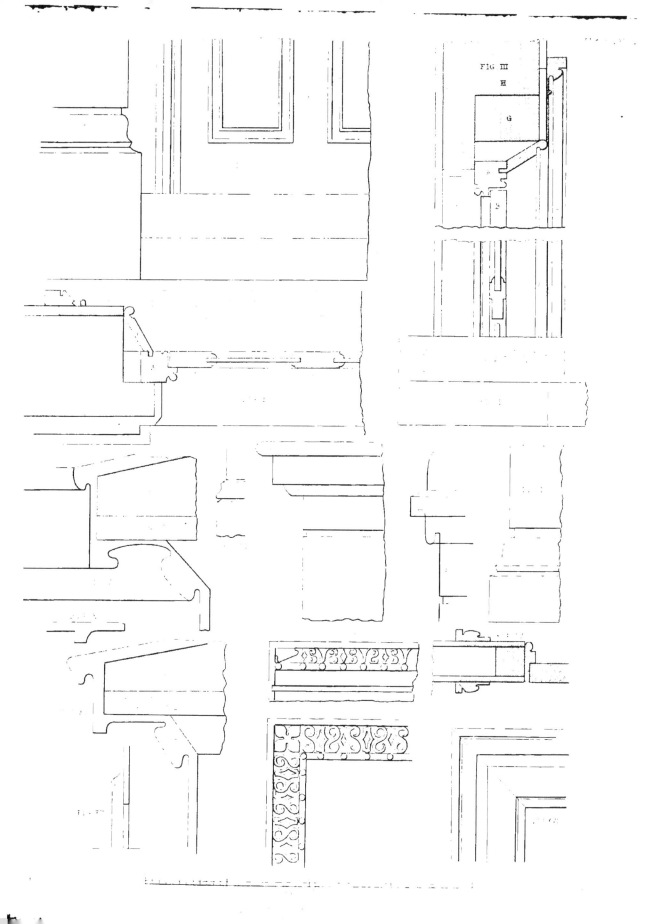

FIG III

117

The rich and decorated Gothic, such as was employed in the minsters of Strasburg and York, the cathedral of Cologne, and many other ecclesiastical structures, too numerous to mention, is not suited to domestic architecture ; but when the embellishments are reduced, and the arrangement of parts is simplified, the style may be employed with great advantage. The difficulty felt by the young artist in applying the Gothic to domestic architecture, is in proportioning those parts which are massive and grand in our churches and cathedrals, to the diminished areas occupied by private edifices, and of forming a pleasing but broken outline which shall stand boldly out against the horizon. A little practice, however, will soon overcome these difficulties, and render the student expert both in the theory and execution of this class of buildings. The next difficulty he will experience will be in giving the doors and windows a suitable proportion, so as to make them, as they should be, important features in the construction, and yet neither too light nor too heavy for the general or individual parts of the design. In nearly all our Gothic churches the entrance doors are deep arches diminishing towards the interior of the building, and are decorated with statues or columns, niches, or other ornaments. This kind of entrance doorway would be most inconsistent if introduced in a cottage or any domestic structure, unless of vast size, and with proportionate boldness in all the details.

In designing the entrance to a Gothic residence, two things are to be considered, the size of the opening and the character of the ornaments. Too often the eye is offended with the sight of doors which do not appear to be a part of the building, but to have been introduced from some after-thought of the architect ; not left when the building was erected, but cut away when all was completed. Nor is it uncommon to see them so entirely destitute of proportion as to occupy nearly one-half of the entire front of the villa, or so small as to produce a feeling that we should be put to inconvenience in entering. In ancient Gothic edifices we have frequent occasion to complain of the exceeding want of propriety in the size of the entrance doors, which often appear as though they were intended to lead to some cold underground apartment, rather than to the richly decorated and magnificent nave of a cathedral. This fault, for such it must be considered, even by those who most admire the works of the ancient Gothic architects, we are accustomed to follow without the slightest consideration. There are many things in which our predecessors have erred, and yet modern artists seem to think they ought to adopt their faults with their beauties, as though they were essential parts of the design. With respect to the height of a door-way, it may be remarked that it should never be less than the stature of the tallest of men. The limit, therefore, is an inch or two more than six feet, and any additional height must be regulated by the artist's conception of the proportion between the door and other parts of the edifice, or of the building as a complete design. The height being fixed, the breadth must be determined, which should never be so contracted as to compel a man to enter in any particular posture. The least breadth that can be allowed is 3 feet, and this, being half the given height, is a good proportion, as far as the door itself is considered; but the relation of its size to the entire building should also be studied.

In designing for a residence in the Gothic style, an architect must also be careful to increase as much as possible, and particularly when his building is rich in its details, the apparent extent of the structure. An irregular plan is for this purpose of much importance, and it has the further advantage of increasing the effect of the design, by throwing deep and broad shadows, and of allowing the architect to give a prominence to the principal apartments. Nothing could offend the eye more than to see a number of gable ends and Gothic decorations introduced upon an uniform front. The horizontal lines must be broken, the projections upon the plan must be considerable, and oriels or bows must be introduced. These few remarks may assist the young artist in designing for Gothic domestic architecture, but we would suggest to him the importance of examining the best specimens of style in connection with the rules we have here laid down. It is singular, and a fact not easily accounted for, that when a person has gained the vaguest possible idea of building, and is just able to distinguish one style from another, he imagines

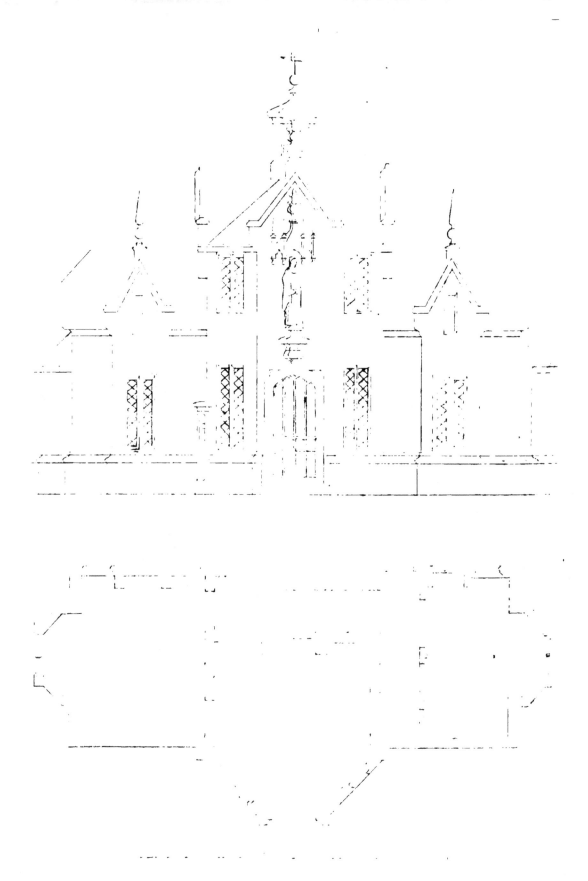

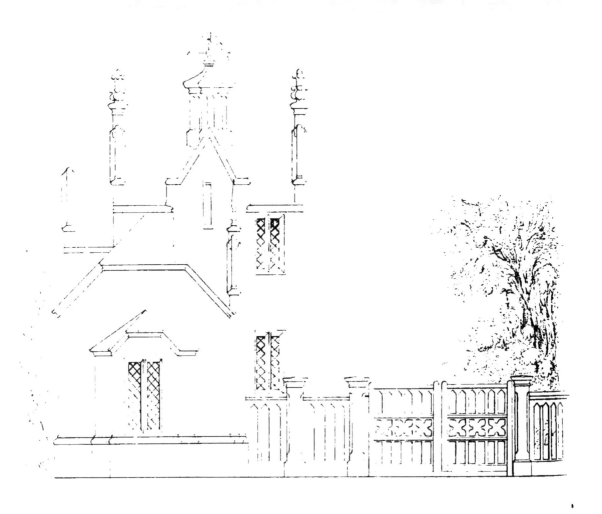

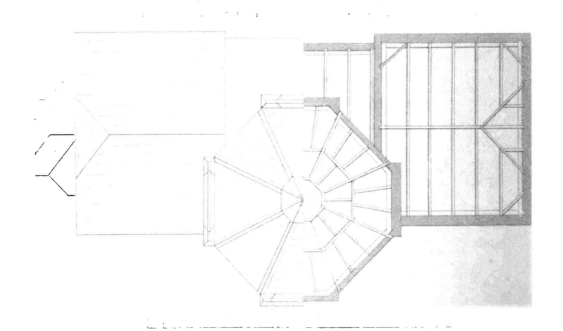

himself to be not only acquainted with the art, but to be able to design and execute his loose and bewildered conceptions. It is true that he soon discovers his mistake; but he has no sooner recovered from the effects of one folly, than he commits another. We believe, that in almost every branch of human knowledge, those who have the most confidence in themselves, and believe themselves to be possessed of most information, are the most ignorant; but on no other subject does the self-assurance carry them to such an extent of absurdity, as to perpetuate their own folly, and to give them so constant a cause of regret, when by an increase of knowledge, they are able to discern the amount of their former ignorance. When a building is once erected, it is a constant character to the constructor, and its beauties or deformities are always associated with his name.

To the young artist, therefore, we cannot sufficiently recommend a close study of all the best examples of architecture, in whatever style he may be designing; to be most careful in regulating the proportions of the several parts of his edifice; but above all to discard all authorities, and while he listens with attention and without prejudice to every opinion, to exercise his own judgment in the selection of the right from the wrong.

Plate LXXXVIII.

Figure 1. Is the front elevation of a cottage in the Gothic style of architecture. This design and the internal arrangements are suited for a game-keeper's residence, or an entrance lodge to a gentleman's park.

Figure 2. Is the ground-floor plan, and consists of a principal room, kitchen and parlour.

Plate LXXXIX.

Figure 1. Is the end elevation.

120

Figure 2. Is a half plan of the roof, showing it when slated, and completely finished.

Figure 3. Is a half plan of the roof, showing the timbers and their bearings on the walls.

Plate XC.

Figure 1.—Cap of gate post to a large scale.

Figure 2.—Capping for top of gate.

Figure 3.—Section of cast metal quarterfoil of gate.

Figure 4.—Elevation of the same.

Figure 5.—Half the elevation of entrance door, showing the external finishings.

Figure 6.—Half the elevation of entrance door, showing the internal finishings.

The dotted lines in figures 5 and 6, show the method of obtaining the centres to strike the arches.

Figure 7.—Section of the door, showing the external and internal finishings.

Figure 8.—The hinge of front door to a large size.

Figure 9.—Plan of entrance door.

Figure 10. Design of an escutcheon for front door; half size.

This building may be erected for about £450.

121

In various parts of this work, allusion has been made to what have been called the five orders; three of which were, as already stated, of Grecian, and two of Roman invention. The orders are chiefly distinguished by the forms and proportions of the column and its entablature, each being divided into three parts. The column consists of a base, a shaft, and a capital: the entablature of an architrave, a frieze, and a cornice. The proportions between all these are regulated according to the order: as they are made up of a number of parts, the form, projection, and face of each must be carefully studied, to obtain an outline and contour suitable to the degree of strength and ornament required; or in other words, the order of architecture.

In Plate XCI. and the two following, we have given a design for a villa in the Ionic order, and it will not be an inappropriate time to describe the general features of that beautiful style, and to notice some of the most remarkable buildings of antiquity in which it was employed. In doing this, however, we shall have occasion to allude to many architectural principles, which would not be understood by the unprofessional or inexperienced reader, had they not been illustrated in the introductory account which precedes the description of Plate LXVII. and the two following.

The capital is the most characteristic feature of the Ionic order. It is distinguished by four spirals, called volutes, two of which are shown on the front, and two on the back face. The projecting fillet is called the hem; the centre of the spiral, the cathetus; and the sunk part the channel. It is remarkable that this very beautiful capital seems to have been more accurately determined in all its proportions, than that of any other order; for there is but little deviation between the several ancient examples which have descended to our own times, and even modern artists follow the ancients with but little alteration in any of the leading characteristics.

The arts are always progressive among a people who are advancing in civilization, and new forms, arrangements, orders, or styles, are invented. So also, when a people have attained great excellence, and begin to pass from a state of luxury to one of vicious and deformed habit, the elegance or beauty which distinguished the early practice of architecture, is changed to tawdry ornament and a neglect of chaste proportion. These statements are proved, without doubt, by the rise of the art in Greece, and its fall in Rome. "The first productions of the arts," says Chambray, "have always been rare, because it is more difficult to invent than to imitate. After the regular buildings, and the famous Doric temples had appeared, of which Vitruvius and some others have made mention, architecture did not long remain in its infancy; the competition and emulation of neighbouring tribes caused it to make great progress in its advance towards perfection. The Ionians were the first who competed with the Dorians in this divine art, and as this people had not the advantage nor glory of its invention, they endeavoured to enrich it more than the Dorians had done."

The proportions first given to the Ionic order, were very different from those adopted in the earliest examples of Doric; the former being eight diameters, and the latter scarcely four. Both these orders, however, were improved by study and observation; so that the specimens of later date are far more elegant and in more accurate proportions, than those of earlier periods.

In the splendid Ionic temple of the Ilissus, the entablature has a height of four modules, sixteen parts; and that of the column sixteen modules. In the entablature, the architrave is one module, twenty-five parts, the frieze one module, nineteen parts; and the cornice one module, two parts.

The entablature of the temple of Erectheus, is four modules, seventeen parts and a half in height. The column is eighteen modules.

The temple of Ilissus is characterised by extreme simplicity. The only ornaments we find in this beautiful specimen of the Ionic are, the oves of the capital, the flutings of the shaft, and the horizontal flutings of the torus in the base. In the temple of the Erectheus, nearly all the mouldings are decorated with sculptured ornaments.

The entablature of the various specimens of Ionic erected by the Romans,

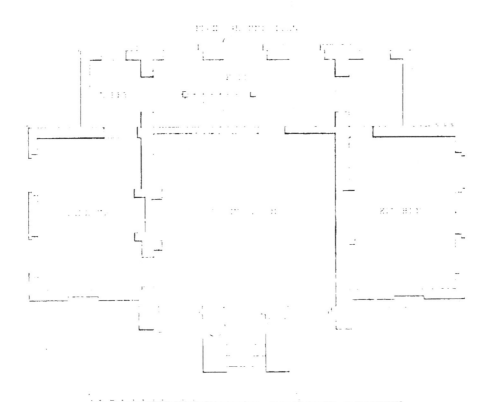

is distinguished from the Grecian, by a greater number of mouldings. "It is easy to prove," says a modern author, "that there exists a strongly marked difference in the composition of the entablature of each order, whether it be in the edifices of Greece, constructed before the time of Augustus, or in those erected at Rome, in the reign of the following emperors. These progressive improvements made in the Ionic ordonnance, have really brought this order to the highest perfection.

The Ionic shaft, like the Doric, is sometimes fluted, but in a different manner. The Doric flutings are segments of a circle, conjoined; while those of the Ionic are of a semi-circular form, and have an intermediate fillet to separate one from the other.

According to common practice, the height of the column should be nine modules or diameters, and of the entablature, two and a quarter. But these proportions are slightly changed according to circumstances, and the taste of the architect.

In the design presented to the public in Plate XCII., we have endeavoured to secure all the beauty of style so remarkably distinguishing the Ionic order, without involving the great expenses necessarily resulting from an introduction of all the splendid ornaments, appropriate for the decorated examples of the order. Our design is one in which all the principles of classic architecture have been exhibited, without regard to ornamental decoration, and with a view to propriety; for that application of the order, which may be suitable for a large public edifice, would be evidently unfit for a small villa.

Plate XCI.

Figure 1. Is the elevation of a design for a cottage in the Grecian style of architecture, and in the Ionic order.

Figure 2. Is the ground plan, consisting of a drawing-room, 18 feet by 16 feet; a parlour, 13 feet by 11 feet; and a kitchen of the same dimensions, with lobby, larder, and convenient staircase. This story should be 9 feet 6 inches high in the clear of the floor-boards and ceiling.

124

Plate XCII.

Figure 1. Is a perspective view of the design.

Figure 2. Is the chamber plan, showing the bed-rooms in the centre of the building, and the roofs of the lower portions or wings.

DETAILS.

Plate XCIII.

Figure 1.—Section of principal cornice.

Figure 2.—Section of string course.

Figure 3.—Base of plinth.

Figure 4.—Cap of antæ.

Figure 5.—Cornice of chimney tops.

Figure 6.—A section of the top and bottom of one of the principal windows, showing a new method of fixing the sash frame to the stone sill; dispensing with the old method of wedging the frame to the oak sill, and that to the stone, rendering the work at the same time more impervious to wind and water.

Figure 7.—A section of the same to a larger scale.

Figure 8.—A perspective view of the back of the frame, showing the cavity left for a stone wedge. A. Boxings for weights. B. Stone sill. C. Cavity for stone wedge, which when filled in, cannot be seen externally. D. Wood coping. E. Stone tenon, upon which the boxing drops.

Figure 9.—Elevation of chimney piece, for drawing-room.

Figure 10.—Plan of the same.

Figure 11.—Section of the same.

Figure 12.—Section of shelf, full size.

Figure 13.—Section of base of pilaster, full size.

Figure 14.—Architrave for principal doors.

Figure 15.—Architrave for windows.

This building may be erected for about £475.

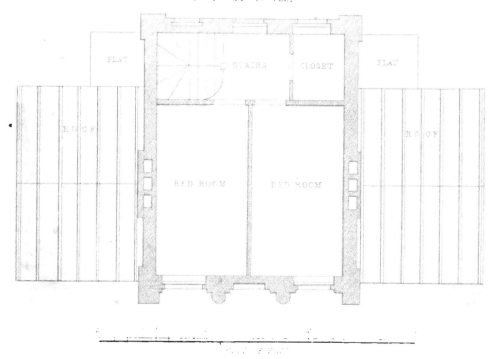

FLAT

STAIRS CLOSET FLAT

ROOF

ROOF

BED ROOM BED ROOM

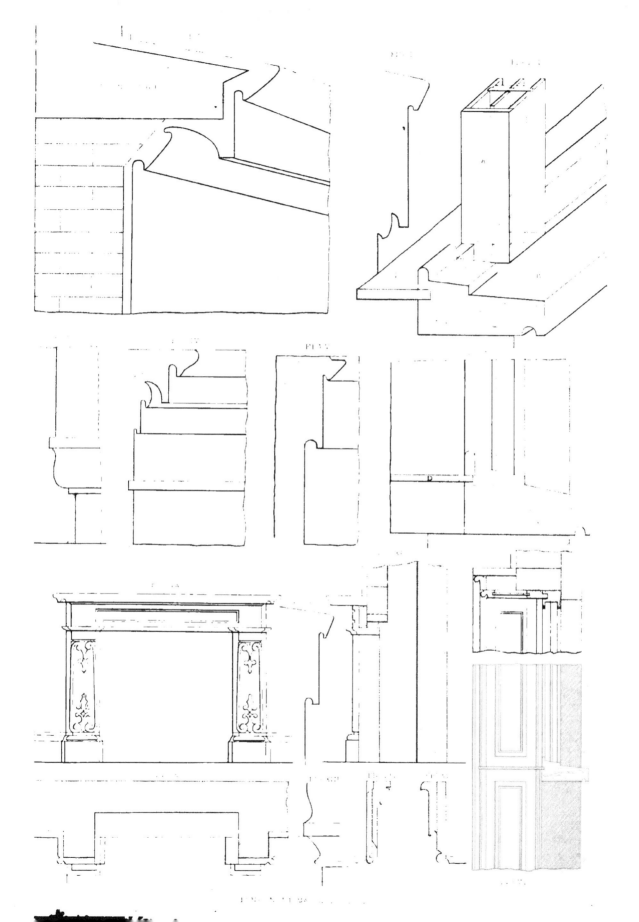

125

· In this work we have not only attempted to describe the various styles of architecture, but have also explained the method of constructing various parts of a building. In the few introductory observations to be here made, we shall endeavour to describe some of the methods which have been adopted for the construction of floors. A floor may be constructed of earth, brick, stone, or wood, but it is of the latter we are about to speak. In common conversation the word floor signifies merely the covering, whether boards or stone, but the builder gives it a much more extensive meaning, and uses it when speaking of the timbers which support the boards. This naked flooring may be of different kinds, according to the size of the room, and other circumstances : thus we have single floors, double floors, and framed floors.

A single floor is one in which there is only one series of timbers called joists. When there is a room below the one in which we are placing our floor, there must be some arrangement for the ceiling. Smaller pieces of wood, therefore, are fixed to the joists, and at right angles to them ; and these, from the purpose for which they are used, are called ceiling joists. It is found to be an advantage in practice, to make every fourth joist deeper than the others, and to fix the ceiling joists to these, as it prevents in some degree the passage of sound. In addition to this the floor should be pugged when it is important to prevent the passage of sound. The process of pugging consists of fixing a boarding between the joists, and spreading over it a coarse kind of mortar.

In a double floor there are two tiers of joists, one called binding joists, the other bridging joists. It is the former that carry the principal weight, and it is upon the upper side of them that the bridging joists are notched, while on the under side they carry the ceiling joists.

A framed floor is constructed in nearly the same manner, except that a large piece of timber called a girder is introduced, and into this the binding joists are framed. In very large rooms, and in places where great weights are to be carried, these girders are necessary, and upon them the strength

2 L

of the floor chiefly depends. Iron is now not unfrequently employed in large buildings, and when judiciously introduced may be a saving of expense and an additional security.

In designing a floor, the first thing to be considered is the bearing; and it must then be remembered that it is the duty of the employed to effect the object desired with the least possible expenditure of time and material. In old houses we are constantly finding a most lavish introduction of timber, and not unfrequently so used as to be absolutely a dead weight upon the walls, and performing no useful office. It has been found by experiment that a single floor will carry a greater weight than a double floor, each having the same amount of timber; but when the bearings are considerable, the ceilings are apt to crack. While, therefore, on the one hand a due attention is given to the saving of expense, a regard to strength must not be omitted, or the work may fail, and a much greater outlay be required to mend imperfections than would have been sufficient to have made the work perfect.

Plate XCIV.

Figure 1. Is a perspective view of a double cottage in the Tudor style of architecture, supposed to be separated from any other buildings; presenting a very picturesque appearance in the exterior, and not wanting in convenience for a small family. Each dwelling is intended to have a kitchen, back kitchen, larder, and water-closet on the basement; a dining-room, 20 feet by 18 feet, a drawing-room of the same dimensions, and a conservatory, 18 feet by 11 feet, on the ground floor; two bed-rooms on the first floor, and servants' rooms in the roof.

Figure 2. Is the ground plan of one of the cottages.

Figure 3. Is the plan of the ground floor, showing the joists, trimmers, &c.

Plate XCV.

Figure 1. Shows the garden front of one of the cottages, with the approach to, and elevation of the conservatory.

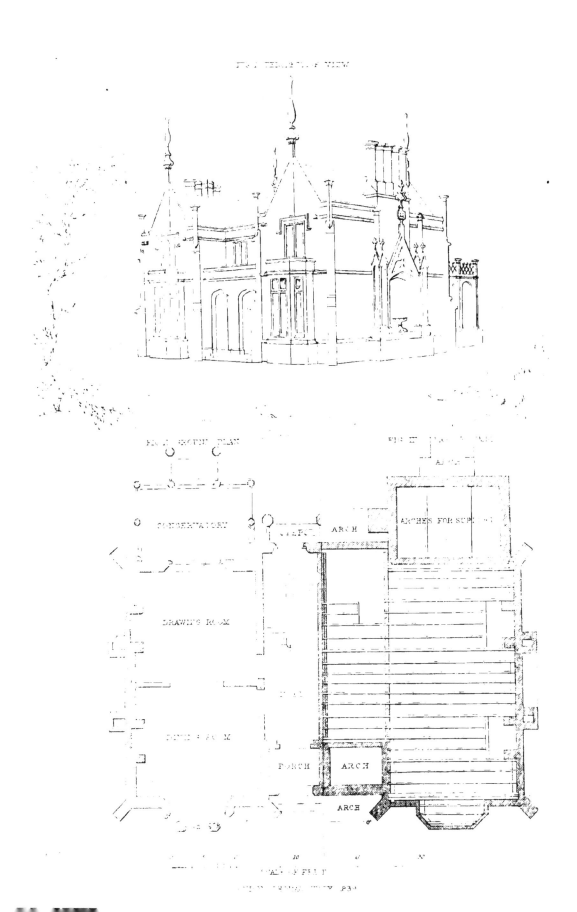

FIG. I. PERSPECTIVE VIEW

FIG. II. GROUND PLAN

FIG. III. CHAMBER PLAN

CONSERVATORY

DRAWING ROOM

STEPS ARCH

ARCHES FOR SUPPORT

DINING ROOM

PORCH ARCH

ARCH

SCALE OF FEET
10

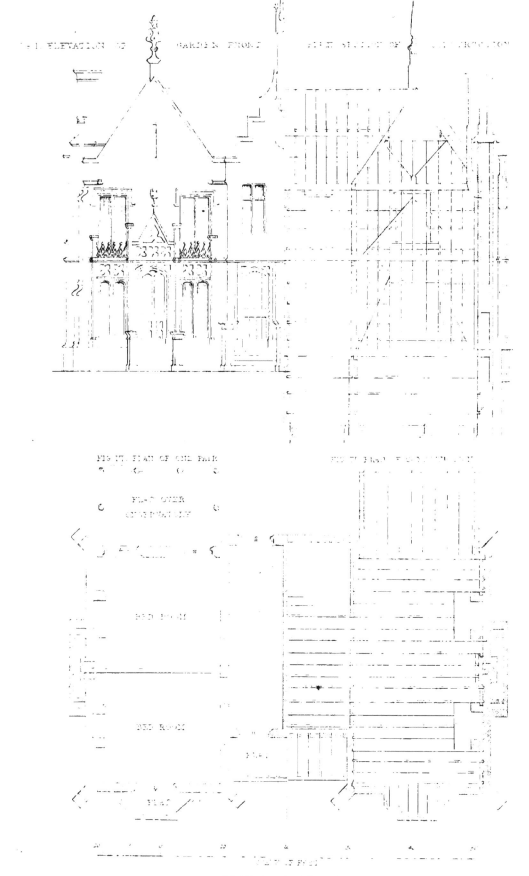

FIG III. PLAN OF ONE PAIR

PLAN OVER
CONSERVATORY

FIG IV. PLAN OF GROUND PLAN

BED ROOM

BED ROOM

HALL

PLAN

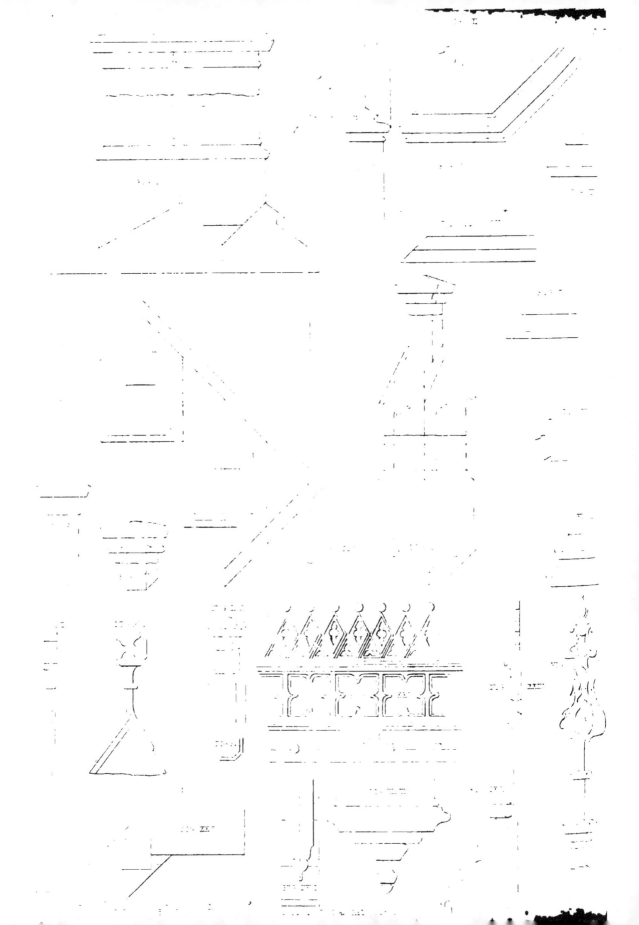

Figure 2. Is a transverse section, showing the construction of the walls, flues, partitions, and roofs.

Figure 3. Is a plan of the first or one pair floor, showing the bed rooms, flats, and staircase.

Figure 4.—Plan showing the construction of the chamber-floor, with the method of laying the joists and trimmers, and the construction of the walls and flues.

DETAILS.

Plate XCVI.

Figure 1. Is an elevation showing the method of finishing the chimney shafts.

Figure 2. Is a plan of the same.

Figure 3.—A section of the diminishing cap for the buttresses.

Figure 4.—The end elevation of the coping for the gable ends.

Figure 5.—The side elevation of the same.

Figure 6.—The plan of the same.

Figure 7.—Section of the string course.

Figure 8.—Section of the coping of the porch and bay windows.

Figure 9.—Elevation of the turret for side and garden fronts.

Figure 10.—Plan of the same.

Figure 11.—Moulding for the plinth to the base of building.

Figure 12.—Section of the label for windows.

Figure 13.—Mouldings for the plinth of the bay windows.

Figure 14.—Plinth for the posts in the elevation of conservatory.

Figure 15.—Cap for the same.

Figure 16.—Cap of post at back entrance.

Figure 17.—Section of finial to gable end of conservatory.

Figure 18.—Elevation of the same.

Figure 19.—Cap and base of porch at entrance of conservatory.

Figure 20.—Plan of the same.

Figure 21.—Design for parapet over front of conservatory, to be cast in zinc.

Figure 22.—Plan of the same.

Figure 23.—Section of the same.

Figure 24.—Elevation of the finials.

Figure 25.—Plan of the method of finishing one of the angular buttresses.

Figure 26.—The elevation of a part of one of the angular buttresses.

Figure 27.—Side elevation of the same.

Figure 28.—The base of the turret to the garden front.

According to our estimate this double cottage may be executed for about the sum of £1,200. It is, however, necessary to state that all our estimates in this work have been given under the supposition that circumstances are favourable. Every one acquainted with building must be perfectly aware that the cost of erecting any edifice must vary according to the relative facility of obtaining materials. In some situations wood may be procured at a low price, and bricks, or stone, having a long carriage, will be expensive. In other instances the reverse of this will be true, while in some situations all materials will be expensive. Hence it is that the cost of erecting a building may be much greater in one place than in another.

Among all the subjects which have been treated of in this work, we have not as yet sufficiently explained the importance of an attention to the heating and ventilating of buildings. It has been casually noticed, but when we consider how much the value and convenience of a house depend upon a sufficiency of heat and air, it seems necessary that we should enter upon the subject more fully. We do not so much propose to ourselves at present, an explanation of the various methods of warming and ventilating, for they are almost innumerable, and the mere mention of them would fill our pages; but rather to direct the attention to principles, for if these be understood, the reader will be able to determine for himself, which plan is best adapted for the purpose, or even invent his own method of accomplishing the end he has in view.

In a country where the changes of temperature are great and sudden, it is most important that we should have some means of raising or diminishing it as may be required. And as, at the same time, all apartments which are inhabited, have, after a period, a deleterious atmosphere, it is important that a convenient method should be provided of discharging the foul air, and admitting pure to supply its place. Now it is an established law of nature, that all vapours expand by heat, or, in other words, become bulk for bulk greater. Thus, supposing the pressures to be equal, air, at the temperature of 32 degrees, does not occupy the same space as when at 80 or 100 degrees. This leads us at once to the fact, that in every apartment the air as it is heated, rises to the top, and the colder portion is at the bottom. There must, therefore, be two currents in every room, one of hot air, attempting to rush out, and one of cold air, rushing in. That this is the case, may be easily proved; for if a person, standing in a room where a fire has been lighted, or a number of persons have been sitting for a long time, place the flame of a candle at the crevice at the top of the door, it will be blown outwards, and at the crevice at the bottom of the door, it will be blown inward; in one case by the hot air which is escaping, in the other by the cold air which is entering. To secure a sufficient and healthy atmosphere, the escape of the hot and deleterious air should be facilitated by the arrangements of the architect; care at the same time being taken that a sufficiently high temperature for health and comfort be preserved.

Now there are two methods of heating the air in an apartment, one a process of radiation, the other of conduction; the latter is the less common, and yet as it is the most evident principle, we will first explain its action. Nearly all substances in nature conduct heat in some degree, but there is a vast difference in their conducting powers; a fact which may be proved by many familiar experiments. Place in a fire a rod of iron and a stick of glass; when that end of the iron which is most distant from the fire, is so hot that it can scarcely be touched by the hand, the same end of the glass will be scarcely warmed. By a similar experiment, though conducted in a more careful manner, and by a more certain test of temperature than the sense of touch, the relative conducting powers of many substances have been determined. Now of all conductors, the metals are the best, and consequently, if they are brought into connection with any body hotter than themselves, they will receive a portion of its heat by conduction. We have an instance of this, in the method of heating buildings by the circulation of hot water, or hot air, in iron pipes. The water being raised to a temperature of 212 degrees, and continually circulating, imparts a considerable amount of its heat to the pipe through which it flows. The air is in contact with the external surface of the pipe, and is also heated by conduction. A certain number of particles of air, if we may so speak, surround the pipe, and receiving an increased temperature by contact, expand and rise. Another series of cold particles then take their place, and in the same manner are heated. It is thus by a rapid change of particles round the centre of heat, that the whole atmosphere is in a short time brought to a higher temperature, and made suitable to the wants or comforts of those who are to live in it. There is one experiment which so beautifully exhibits the conductive powers of metals, that we cannot resist the temptation to mention it. Take a rod of metal and a stick of charcoal; round the end of each, wrap *tightly* a piece of writing

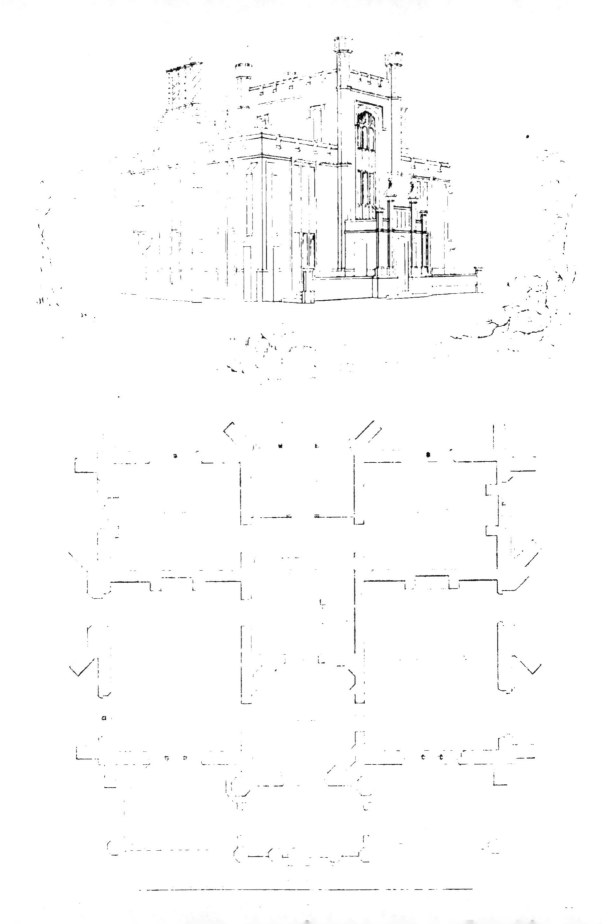

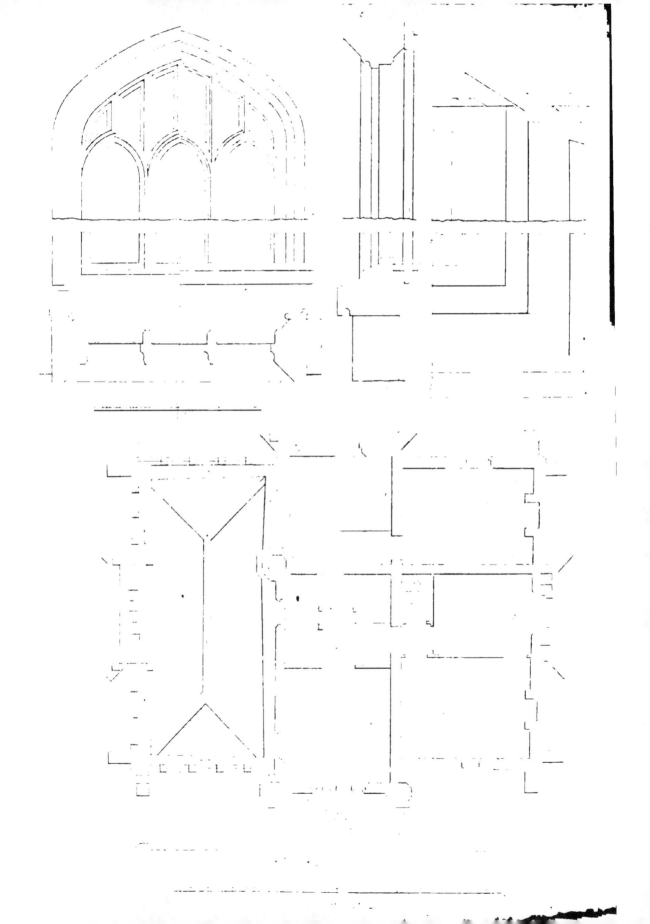

paper; place the paper on each of these, in the flame of a candle, and that which is twisted round the charcoal, (which is a bad conductor,) is soon burnt. But the paper round the metal is not burnt, or even singed, because the heat is conducted away by the metal.

We shall renew this subject in the next description.

Plate XCVII.

Figure 1. Is the perspective view of a design for a villa, in the modern style of Gothic Architecture, and suited for the residence of a man of distinction or large property.

Figure 2. Is the ground plan of the same, consisting of an entrance porch 15 feet, by 6 feet, communicating with an octagonal entrance hall, 12 feet in diameter, leading to a dining-room, 20 feet by 16 feet, and a drawing-room of the same dimensions. In the second, or interior hall, there is a grand staircase to the bed-rooms; and in the back part of the house two sitting-rooms, 15 feet by 14 feet, one to be used as a library, the other as a breakfast-room. The kitchens and domestic apartments are supposed to be in the basement.

Plate XCVIII.

Figure 1. Is the detail of the top of the large window over the porch.

Figure 2. Is the bottom portion of the same.

One half of the elevation of this window exhibits the appearance externally, and the other half internally, with the method of finding the centres to turn the arches.

Figure 3. Is a plan of the same window.

Figure 4. Is a section, showing the head and sill of the same.

132

Figure 5. Is a perspective sketch of one of the stone mullions, showing the method of fixing and hanging the cast metal casements.

Figure 6. Shows the same mullion upon the sill.

Figure 7. Is a plan of one half of the building, showing the roof over the lower portion, the stairs, bed-room, and a part of the roof of the central building.

Figure 8. Shows a half plan of the first pair, or principal chamber floor, which consists of six good sized bed-rooms, and two dressing-rooms. All these are suited to the character of the house, and are so designed, that they would be both spacious and airy.

Plate XCIX.

Figure 1. Is the half elevation of the exterior of the entrance porch.

Figure 2. Is the half elevation of the interior of the entrance porch. We have also so made the drawing, that it will equally serve the purpose of a section.

Figure 3. Is a plan of the foundations of tower and porch.

Figure 4. Is a plan of the same on the floor line.

The door and door-frame may be framed and fixed in the manner explained in the description of a design in the Tudor style.

The ground floor of this building should be, when finished, 12 feet high, the second floor 10 feet, and the attics 8 feet 6 inches.

It is supposed that the whole of the work may be executed in the best style, for about £2,500.

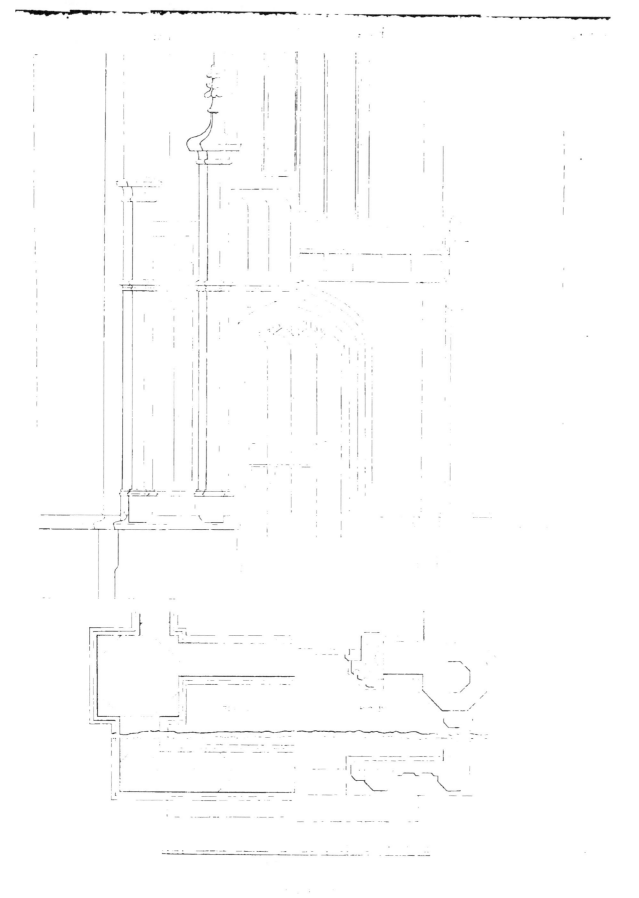

133

In our introductory essay to the description of Plates XCVII., XCVIII., and XCIX., we commenced an investigation of the principles of heating and ventilating, which we shall now conclude. In that part of our essay we stated a few facts regarding the effect produced upon air by an increase of temperature, and stated that heat may be communicated from one body to another, by conduction and radiation. Of the conduction of heat we have an excellent example in the system of heating buildings by hot water or steam circulating through metallic pipes. All hot-air stoves produce their effects by the principle of conduction; for air being made to circulate through a space in which it is acted upon by some source of heat, escapes into the apartment in which they are placed at a temperature much higher than that it has under common circumstances.

But we will now proceed to explain what is meant by the radiation of heat, and illustrate the application of the principle in warming buildings. When we stand before, but at a considerable distance from a coal fire, we are sensible of receiving heat from it, and yet there is no conduction, and, in fact, no conducting medium. It is true that there is atmospheric air between us and the fire, but it is not, as is most evident, the medium of communication. Heated air, as we have already stated, rises, and does not proceed in horizontal lines; besides which, the heat received is but partially felt, for it is only that portion of our bodies exposed to the fire that receives the heat, and we may so place ourselves that although the one part of the body exposed to the fire may be painfully affected, the other parts may be excessively cold. But as these remarks may not be sufficient in the estimation of some persons, to prove that the heat received is not by the conduction of the air, we may further state that heat may be communicated from one body to another in a vacuum. This has been proved by a variety of beautiful and delicate philosophical experiments, which cannot be described with propriety in this article, but of the truth of which our readers may be satisfied by reference to any work upon the science of heat.

The system of warming buildings generally adopted in this country, is that of radiation, and consequently deserves some attention from us. The method of placing a coal fire in an iron grate, immediately under a flue, which is necessary for carrying away the smoke, is as well suited to prevent the warming of an apartment by conduction as though it were invented for the purpose. The object we have in view in all cases, is to raise the temperature of the air; and this cannot possibly be effected by a coal fire, as usually fixed in the apartments of our houses. The air in a room is constantly forcing itself upon the source of heat, but as it rises by an increase of temperature, it escapes up the flue, and not into the room, causing a fresh accession of cold air, and, therefore, not warming the atmosphere. It is true that a small portion of the heated air may find its way into the room, and that after several hours a convenient and comfortable temperature may be obtained. But if a man should come, cold and tired, into a room in which there was a large fire, but with a wire guard before it, he would, as the result of experience, remove it immediately. Why? we would ask. Not because it prevents the communication of heat by conduction, for if conduction were the only agent he need not go near the fire, or at least the wire guard would not prevent him from receiving all the heat that could be communicated by the heated air proceeding from the fire. The reason is that he is warmed by the radiation of heat, and radiated heat may be absorbed or reflected. All the heat we receive from the sun is by radiation; and we well know that the accumulations of vapour in the atmosphere retard its progress, so that we do not enjoy an equal temperature when the sky is overclouded, as when the atmosphere is clear.

Radiation, or the throwing off in rays, is, then, a principle altogether distinct from conduction; of its advantages in practice as a means of warming buildings, we leave the reader to judge. There are objections and advantages, for although it does not impart the equality of temperature which may be obtained from conduction, we are not sure that an equality is the most enviable state; and our prejudices and recollections are on its side, which some may say are of no value, but which we are not inclined in this instance to disturb.

But we must now come to the conclusion of this subject. A room, whether heated by conduction or radiation, may be too hot, and when a number of persons are in it for a long period may also become unwholesome from the consumption of oxygen. Means must, therefore, be adopted, to regulate the temperature, and to give vent to the heated air, or noxious light gases, which is done by various systems of ventilation. To determine which is most suited to the purpose, the reader must refer to, and judge by the principles stated in this and the preceding essay.

Plate C.

Figure 1.—A perspective view of a small residence, or parsonage-house, in the Grecian style of architecture.

Figure 2.—The principal, or ground plan, consisting of an entrance hall, 13 feet by 6 feet, communicating with the several rooms, and a convenient staircase and conservatory. The height of the dining or drawing-room should be 14 feet; that of the smaller rooms, 9 feet 6 inches.

The chamber floor may be divided in any way to suit the convenience of the proprietor, care being taken not to interfere with the principal walls. The kitchen and domestic offices may be placed either under this story, or on the same level, according to the wish of the person who may build.

Plate CI.

Figure 1. Is the elevation of the garden front, showing the conservatory.

Figure 2. Is the plan of the window of the principal room, showing a new method of attaching metal shutters, so that they may fold round rollers when in their boxings, and when closed will have the appearance of Venetian blinds.

Figure 3. Is the half elevation of the window with the boxings.

Figure 4. Is a half elevation of the same with the shutters closed.

Figure 5.—A section of the window, on which is shown the principle of construction.

Plate CII.

Figure 1. Is the plan of the principal room, with four elevations, showing the method of finishing.

Figure 2. Is a section of the coved cornice and ceiling to a large scale.

Figure 3.—Cap of antæ.

Figure 4.—Base of the same.

Figure 5.—Large external cornice with bracket.

Figure 6.—Ornament for the middle of ceiling in principal room.

Figure 7.—External cornice for the wings of the building.

Figure 8.—Surbase moulding for the rooms on the ground floor.

Figure 9. Shows the method of tracing the angular bracket for the cove of ceiling.

It is estimated that this building may be erected for about £750.

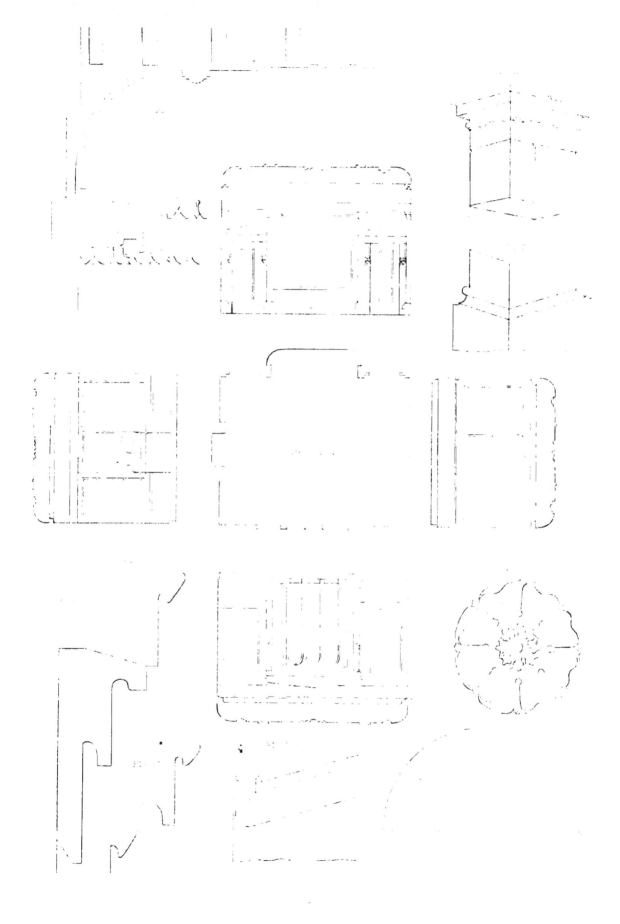

In the preparation of this work, the author has had many objects in view, and has addressed himself to many classes of persons. But there are those (and to them the book will be especially useful,) who may derive from it the elements of their intended profession; and for their benefit we must now make a few remarks, calculated to direct their studies, and aid them in their pursuits. There are few who have arrived at the age of maturity, and entered upon the business of life, who have not occasion to regret either a want of sufficient attention to their studies, or an injudicious system of acquiring knowledge in the early, and, if we may so speak, in the initiatory stage of active mental existence. As soon as men are conscious of the error they have committed, or of the evils which have resulted from a want of experience, they are, as it were, possessed with a desire to guard others from the same cause of future regret. Indolence can only be cured by the person who is afflicted by it, and the production of a more healthy state of mind; but it is in the power of one who has gained a certain advanced stage in the knowledge of a science, to direct the energies of one who is but commencing his studies, and this we shall attempt to do, but more particularly in reference to our own book.

The "Villa Architecture" will not, certainly, be less interesting or valuable to the student, than to the professed architect and the builder. To them our designs are offered as suggestions, but to the student they are presented with still more confidence, as guides, specimens of his art, which, without egotism, we may be allowed to say, he may study with some advantage.

As exercises in the particular style of drawing in which the student is to make himself proficient, the book will be valuable. Here he will find every class of drawing that he can be called upon to perform—perspective views, elevations, plans, and details. Indeed, it would be almost impossible for any person to copy, carefully, and with a studious regard to construction, the plates in this book, without obtaining a considerable facility in architectural drawing. If this plan be carried out with regularity, the advantage will soon be experienced.

The work will also recommend itself to the young, as an explanation of the system of construction adopted by scientific architects in this country. There is scarcely any part of a building which has not been carefully delineated in this work, so that from one or more examples the student may know how any other work of a similar character is to be effected. So fully has this been carried out, that we are unable to conjecture any difficulty which has not been, in some degree, anticipated.

But as soon as a person has obtained a knowledge of the art of drawing, and an acquaintance with the mere elements of construction, he will feel a desire to design, and probably make the attempt. This period in the professional history of a student is always of momentous importance, for he will then lay the foundation of his professional character, and the subsequent practice of the system he may adopt, will make him either a copyist, or an original designer. We have known persons who, when they design, invariably take some design or sketch executed or proposed by another, and alter it, seldom for the better, rather than make an attempt upon their own resources. Ashamed to take a published design, they contort it to make it their own, and introduce many incongruities for the sake of having something different. We, therefore, warn the student of this practice, and urge upon him an independence of feeling and habit. His first designs will probably be such as he cannot himself praise, but a decided and persevering effort will overcome all difficulties, and after a few trials he will not only be better pleased with his performances, but also gain confidence. Here also he is in danger. Nothing is more difficult than to sustain a medium between a proper self-confidence, and presumption; and nothing can be more offensive than a cynical spirit towards others, and an overweening pride of ourselves.

The great art of designing in architecture is to maintain a unity of effect, and the most accurate proportions. It should always be remembered that a building is to be looked upon as a whole, as well as in its parts. It is not impossible to imagine a structure so perfect in every detail, that when examined in this way, it may be deserving of the highest praise, and yet when

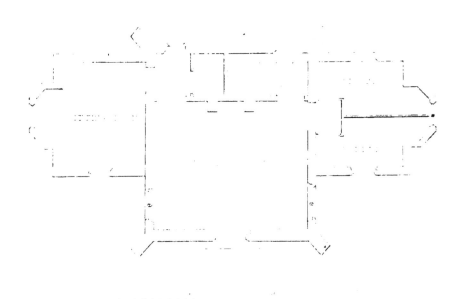

viewed as a whole, may be grotesque or ridiculous. It is therefore important beyond all estimate, that the draughtsman should have a clear perception of the building he intends to construct, view it in every position, and make all the details subserve to the production of the effect he has in view. Gross blunders are made, and disgusting edifices are occasionally reared, from want of a sufficient attention to this important rule. What can be the sense of propriety, order, design, taste, nay, what can be his power of reflection, who makes a Gothic exterior for a private residence, and finishes the interior in a bastard Grecian style? and yet this has occurred in a thousand instances. There is not the same objection to a Gothic room, particularly a library, in a residence which is strictly classical, provided the Gothic character of architecture be confined to the area it occupies, and be not perceptible from any point of view. It is then perfect in itself, and being viewed as a construction complete in itself, must be calculated to please rather than offend. Still, if but a Gothic window-frame and sash can be seen from without, it is not only objectionable, but a reproach to the architect. There are some persons, who, preferring the Grecian, Roman, or our own domestic style, to any other, for their residences, desire to have one or more apartments with Gothic decorations; and if this be required, those apartments should always be so placed that they may not make a part of the general elevation, or even be seen at the same time, unless they can be lighted from above. This is but one instance among many which might be mentioned, to show the necessity of unity in every design, and of making every part subservient to one object. In all our sketches we have endeavoured to give practical illustrations of this fundamental principle of the science of architecture; and it may be observed in the design to which this essay is prefixed, as well as all others.

Plate CIII.

Figure 1.—A perspective view of a design for a lodge; and equally suited for a country toll-gate. The principal room would probably be found exceedingly convenient as a proper place of meeting for the commissioners in some parts of the country, distant from any town.

140

Figure 2.—The ground plan, consisting of a principal room 19 feet by 15 feet; a sitting-room 12 by 14, including the bow, and suitable cellar and larder.

Plate CIV.

Figure 1. Is a geometrical drawing of the back elevation.

Figure 2. Is a plan of the first floor, showing the bed-room and roofs over the small buildings.

DETAILS.

Plate CV.

Figure 1.—The external elevation of the bay windows.

Figure 2.—Inside elevation of the same.

Figure 3.—Transverse section.

Figure 4.—Plan of window without the finishings.

Figure 5.—The same with the finishings.

Figure 6.—The elevation of the label over entrance door.

It is estimated that this design may be executed for about £300.

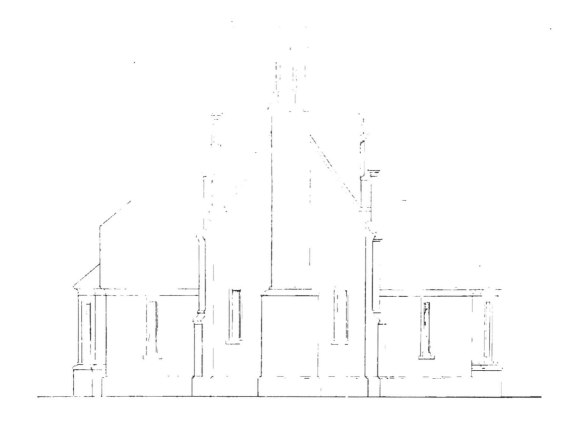

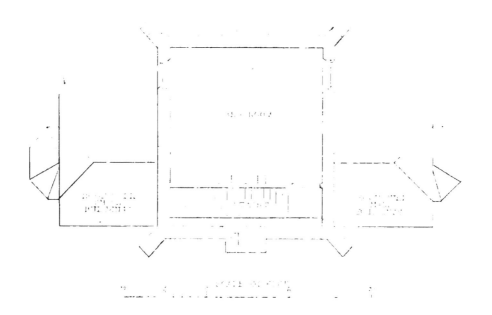

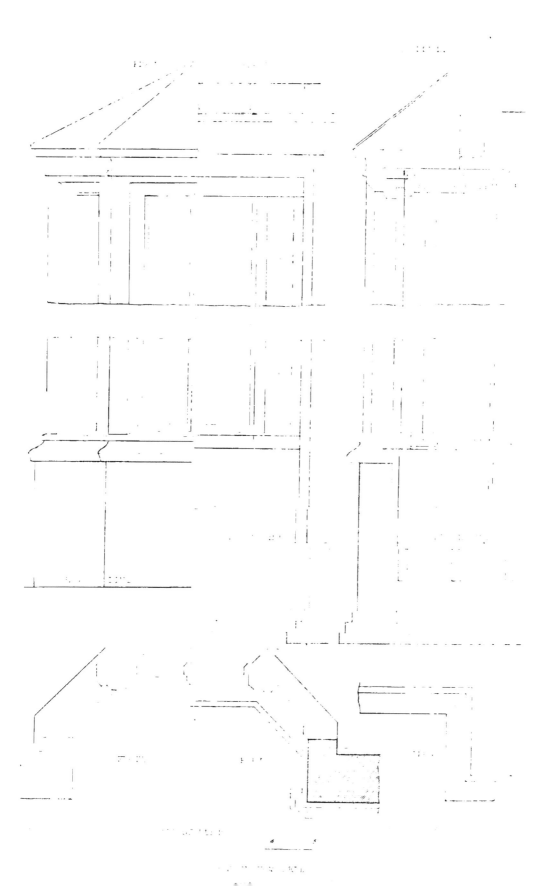

141

Foreigners are always pleased with the elegance and comfort of our villa architecture, and the magnificence of our domestic mansions; but charge us with a great want of taste in supplying those decorations to our pleasure grounds which are equally desirable for comfort and elegance. To this charge we must in candour plead guilty. There is, perhaps, no nation which pays less attention to what may be called the architectural decoration of gardens and pleasure grounds. A rude erection, to which one is puzzled to give a name, which serves the double purpose of a tool-house and an uncertain protection from any sudden violence of the atmosphere, is all that is thought necessary. If, perchance, there should be a summer-house fit for a person to sit in, it is most likely to be such an one as would be a disgrace to the skill, judgment, and taste, of many a wandering savage. The reason of this indifference to the decoration and convenience of our gardens may, we think, be easily discovered. The climate of this country is exceedingly changeable, which prevents the inhabitants from living so much in the air as they would otherwise do. Hence it is that they surround themselves with what we may call in-door comforts, and are by habit so much attached to these, that the pleasure they derive from their gardens and grounds is chiefly the sight of them from the house which they surround. Thus it is they are led to neglect the erection of those elegant and inexpensive structures which make a garden pleasant at all seasons, and repay the labour and cost it always entails upon the proprietor.

Anxious to correct, as far as possible, this inattention to the comfort and usefulness of a garden, we shall endeavour to explain the manner in which we may introduce a better system, the styles which may be adopted, and the methods of construction.

The English people are really attached to their gardens, although they do not know how to enjoy them. They visit them as the curious go to an exhibition—for an hour's amusement, and not as places which may be considered the finest schools for moral and intellectual improvement. A garden is constantly offering some fresh object of study, while it gratifies every sense worthy of cultivation. It is only by inculcating these facts, that men who live in retired situations and possess an opportunity of enjoying nature, can be induced to seek all the pleasure it is calculated to afford.

The erections required in gardens and pleasure grounds are not numerous; but in designing them, more care is required than perhaps in any other kind of building. The doctrine so often enforced in this work, that every structure should be in harmony with the site in which it is placed, applies in its greatest force to garden architecture. The smallest possible structure, even though intended for inferior uses, is not beneath the attention of the architect; for wherever placed, it may be made to give an additional beauty; whereas, if executed without design, or in an inappropriate style, it will appear ridiculous, and even diminish the pleasure with which we view the works of creation, aided as they are in our richly cultivated gardens, by the most wonderful exhibitions of science and art. It is not always necessary that all the garden structures should be in the same style; for as it is but seldom that any two can be seen at the same time, they may be better appropriated to particular situations. The pointed styles are for the most part to be preferred; but the Grecian, and even the rustic, are sometimes to be chosen.

The method of constructing the various edifices, if such we can call them, required in gardens and pleasure grounds, is also a matter of great importance; for there are but few persons who are willing to expend upon them a large sum of money. This circumstance often induces a builder to erect them in the most paltry manner, so that, after a year or two, they are literally a disgrace to the places they were intended to decorate. Brick or stone buildings are always to be preferred, in point of durability, and, generally, of appearance; and yet timber may be often so applied as to last unimpaired for many years, if proper care be taken in the selection of the material, and in keeping it well covered with some substance which will defend it from the weather. There is a class of workmen, and, we fear, of architects also, who are

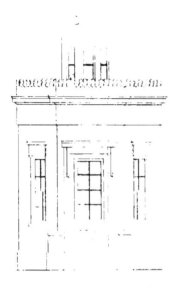

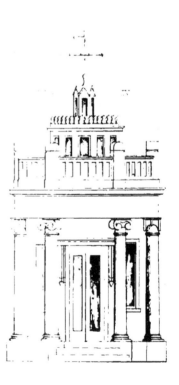

perfectly regardless of the future appearance of the structures they design, or superintend. This indifference to the interest of the proprietor causes them to erect buildings at a low price, which, for a time, are pleasing to the eye, and appear sound in construction; but, after a few years, absolutely fall to pieces. This is especially the case in gardens and pleasure grounds. It should, however, be always remembered by both the builder and employer, that "it is better to leave a thing undone than to do it badly."

Plate CVI.

Figure 1. Is a design for a summer-house octagonal on the plan, and in the Gothic style. This design may be executed for about £25.

Figure 2. Is a design for a similar building in the rustic style. It may be completed for about £15.

Figure 3. Is a design of a similar description in a style which is in part Grecian, and may be built for £30.

Figure 4. Is a design in the Venetian, or, as it is sometimes called, the verandah style, and like all the others, octagonal on the plan. To erect it, would cost about £20.

As all these buildings are exceedingly simple, it has not been thought necessary to give any details, or even the plans.

Plate CVII.

The designs upon this plate are of a higher class than those already given, and have been called pavilions. They are used for the same purposes as the summer-house; but they may also be employed for many others. Either of the buildings we have designed would make a convenient studio, or a place of retreat in the heat of the day or in the cool of the evening; and would, at the same time, be highly decorative and pleasing objects for a gentleman's pleasure grounds.

Figure 1. Is a design for an octagonal pavilion in the plain Grecian style, and may be erected for about the sum of £60.

Figure 2. Is a design in the Ionic style, and square on the plan; and would cost in execution about £150.

Figure 3. Is a design in the Grecian style, more simple in its character and outline than the preceding, which would cost in building about £100.

Figure 4. Is a design in the Ionic style, and more ornamental than either of the others. It is circular on the plan, and would form a pretty object, either in a garden or pleasure ground. The internal appearance of this building would be greatly improved, if a fountain were placed in the centre, surrounded by plants. It is also well adapted for any eminence commanding an extensive or interesting landscape, as windows are introduced between the columns entirely round the building.

Plate CVIII.

This plate contains four plans of the preceding design, each being numbered the same as the design to which it belongs.

All these designs are intended to be built of brick and finished in compo, or of stone, if the situation admits of the use of that material. The floors are to be laid with deal, and the walls may be either painted or papered according to the taste of the proprietor.

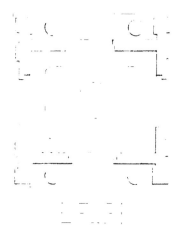

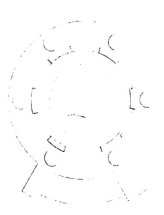

Having now completed our series of designs for cottage and villa architecture, it is our first duty to acknowledge the kind reception of our work, and the patronage bestowed upon it. Our object throughout has been to prepare such a series of drawings as should convey a few hints to the architect, direct the builder, and instruct those who intended to build; and we trust from the manner in which the work has been received by the public, that we have not altogether failed in our attempt.

We will here take the liberty to make a few remarks concerning the employment of architects in designing buildings and superintending their construction. We heard a gentleman of well-known skill state, not long since, that the Villa Architecture was one of that class of books most calculated to injure the profession to which we both belonged. Had we entertained the same opinion, it would not, of course, have been published, how desirous soever we may be to improve the taste of all classes of the community. But with as much propriety might it be said that the publication of a volume of sermons would prevent those who bought it from attendance upon church, or that the reading of a family receipt-book would prevent an application to a medical practitioner in the event of illness. It is true that a builder can understand the designs, details, and construction, so far as they are shown in our drawings, as well as the architect; and hence it may be said that the cases are not parallel. To this objection we must enter our protest. An untutored man, or even one who possesses a certain amount of practical information, but destitute of those advantages derived from the knowledge and experience of others, may pretend to be infallible and to cure all diseases; but no judicious person will, in the event of sickness, trust himself in his hands. There are also some builders who pretend to the art of design, and put forward their capabilities as if they were, and perhaps with the opinion that they are, equal or superior to the most eminent architects of the age; but no one desiring to build with taste will believe that they can be equally as capable of designing as the man whose life has been spent in gathering from the records of all ages and the spirit of poetry, a capability of applying and conceiving forms of elegance and beauty. We may also remark that it is only the man who intends to do a wrong, who can recommend the execution of any work without the superintendence of an architect, except in those cases where professional assistance cannot be obtained without a disproportionate expenditure of capital and time. For whom then, it may be asked, is this work intended? And we reply, for the gentleman, the architect, and the builder. It will assist the gentleman in fixing upon the style in which he will build, the architect it may aid in designing, and the builder in construction; and at the same time be the means of introducing a better style of architecture in those situations where professional assistance cannot be obtained.

We are far from having the opinion which is too common among professional men, that the publication of designs, with their details, will cause those who intend to build to assume the superintendence themselves, and to erect some published sketch which may happen to please their fancy. The more the public taste is improved, the more demand will there be for the assistance of architects. It is a fact which must have been observed by every one, that when an elegant or tasteful building has been erected in any district, men of property begin to think how they can improve their own residences, and the talent of the architect will be required. Such, we hope and believe, will be the result of our work—that it will aid in improving and cultivating a taste for architectural design, and cause many an elegant structure to be erected on sites that are now occupied by bare walls of brickwork.

This work, however, differs from all others not only in the circumstance of its giving the details, both ornamental and constructive, of the designs, but also in presenting to the subscribers an abstract of nearly all the principal subjects of architectural science. Within the space of four pages, attached to each set of drawings, we have not only given a written description, which may be said to be a kind of specification, but also an essay on some branch of architecture or building. In this way we have endeavoured to convey to the reader much useful information on the distinguishing characters of styles, the

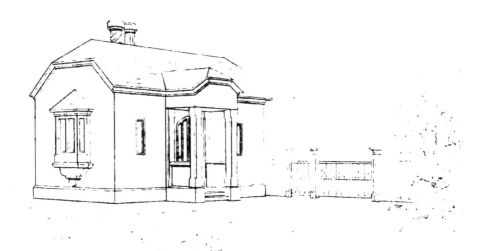

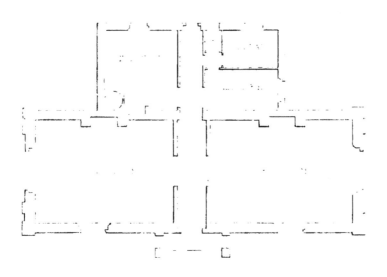

ages in which they were introduced, the improvements that have been effected, and the situations in which they may be most appropriately introduced. We have also endeavoured to disabuse the mind of the notion that architecture is a contracted and illiberal art, in which one student imitates another without any exercise of independent genius or talent, and to place it in its just relation to painting and sculpture. We have explained the proportions of the Grecian orders, and have pointed out how far we are compelled to adopt them as representatives of qualities, and how free the imagination is then left in designing. We have, in fact, been anxious so to place both the science and the art before the public, that a noble and liberal pursuit may no longer be esteemed one which is to be followed, or one in which proficiency can be obtained, without great labour, study, and natural talent. Strange as it may appear, there are many gentlemen of wealth and family who are altogether ignorant of the duties of an architect, and express their surprise when they discover that a man of education is required for successful practice : a fact which may be in a great measure accounted for from the indisposition of the profession to communicate suitable knowledge in books.

Plate CIX.

Figure 1. Is a perspective view of a design in the Tudor style, for a lodge and gate suited for the entrance to a gentleman's grounds.

Figure 2. Is a perspective view of another design for the same purpose.

Plate CX.

Figure 1. Is a perspective view of a third design for a lodge and gate, but in the classical style. All these are applicable to the same plan. To determine which would be most suitable for a certain situation, the taste of the proprietor, and the greater fitness of one than another, must be considered.

Figure 2. Is the ground plan suited to either of the three designs, and consists of a sitting-room, 16 feet 6 inches by 12 feet, a bed-room of the same size, a kitchen, 9 feet 6 inches by 9 feet, a larder, and a cellar.

Plate CXI.

This plate contains the details of gates suited for the three designs.

Figure 1. Is the elevation of two designs for a gate suited to either of the first two perspective views. It is intended to construct it with wood posts fixed upon stone plinths. The hanging posts of the gates may be framed in wood, and the open work may be cast in iron. Gates made in this manner are cheap, and have an exceedingly pretty appearance. AAA. Wood posts. BBB. Stone plinths. CCC. Gate posts. DDD. Cast iron panels.

Figure 2.—Plan of gates. AAA. Posts. BBB. Stone plinths. CCC. Metal panels.

Figure 3. Is a section of the same.

Figure 4. Is a design for a gate suitable for the Grecian lodge. In this case it will be necessary to introduce stone posts and cast metal plates, to correspond with the style of building.

Figure 5. Is a plan of the same.

Figure 6. Is a section of the same.

Either of these designs with the gates complete, may be erected for about the sum of £250.

Printed by J. Rider, 14, Bartholomew Close, London.

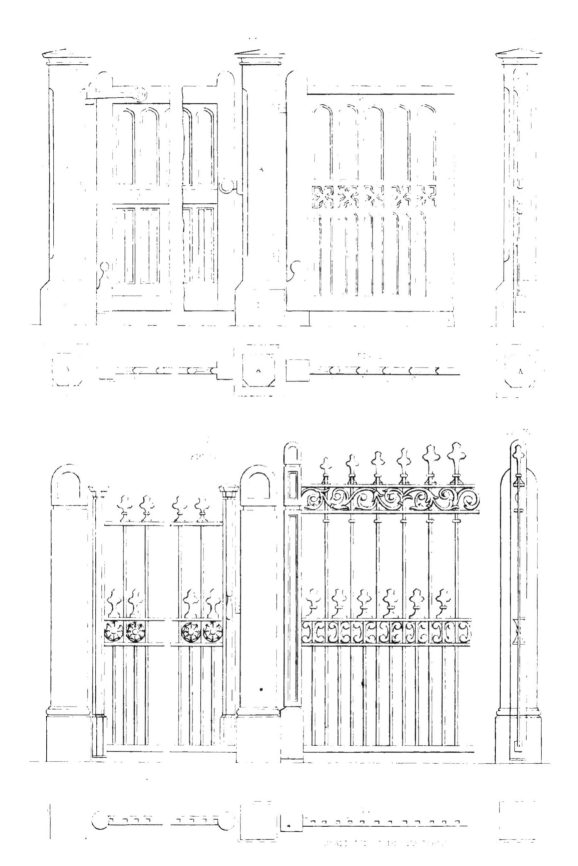

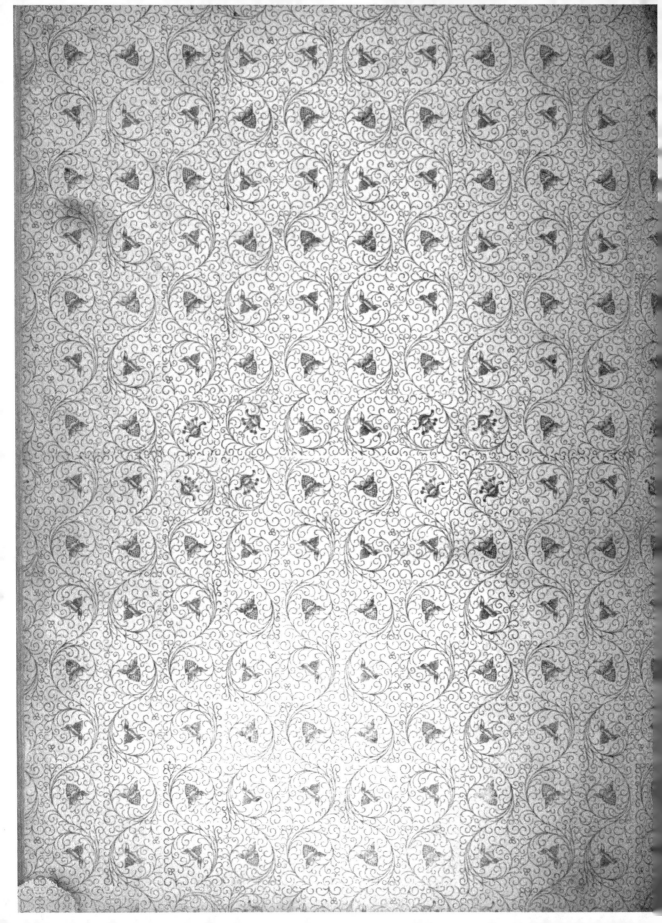

Printed in the USA
CPSIA information can be obtained
at www.ICGtesting.com
CBHW081640170824
13348CB00011B/385